COVENANT RIGHT PRAYERS OF DECLARATION

That Can Change Your Life

FATAI KASALI

30 COVENANT RIGHT PRAYERS OF DECLARATION
That Can Change Your Life

© 2024 Fatai Kasali

The author has asserted his right to be identified as the author of this work in accordance with the Copyright, Designs and Patents Act 1988.

All rights reserved. No part of this publication may be reproduced, stored in a retrieval system, or transmitted, in any form or by any means, electronic, mechanical, photocopying, recording or otherwise without the prior permission of the author.

All Scripture quotations, unless otherwise indicated, are taken from the Holy Bible, King James Version, Cambridge University Press, Oxford University Press, Harper Collins, and the Queen's Printers.

Published in the United Kingdom by Glory Publishing

ISBN: 978-1-9996849-9-0

ACKNOWLEDGEMENTS

To God be the glory for the grace to write this book. I give God all the praise and adoration for giving me the inspiration through His Spirit. This has made possible the writing of this book.

I want to appreciate my family and all those who have contributed one way or the other to the beauty of this work thank you very much. May God Almighty bless you all.

INTRODUCTION

EXODUS 2:24 (KJV): *And God heard their groaning, and God remembered his covenant with Abraham, with Isaac, and with Jacob.*

When the Israelites were in bondage and under the oppression of Egyptians, they started crying, and God heard their cry. He remembered His covenant with their forefathers. This also made God remember the token of that covenant, which guaranteed the right to deliverance for Israel.

Therefore, God arose to grant Israel their covenant right by delivering them from the captivity of the Egyptians.

This implies that when you find yourself in a terrible situation, it is time to arise and claim your covenant rights under the covenant God signed with Abraham (you are the seed of Abraham by faith). You are also a partaker of the new covenant brought into existence by the Lord Jesus Christ.

The Bible details your covenant rights, and it is your responsibility to arise and claim those rights. This book contains 30 powerful prayers of declaration developed from the word of God.

Each of the prayers of declaration addresses your rights in certain situations. Whenever you face a certain situation, declare the word of this declaration to it, and you will experience the miraculous power of your covenant right through these prayers.

CONTENTS

Chapter 1:
Covenant Right Declaration to Divine Peace 11

Chapter 2:
Covenant Right Declaration to A Long Life 15

Chapter 3:
Covenant Right Declaration for Stability 19

Chapter 4:
Covenant Right Declaration to Declare Good Expectations 23

Chapter 5:
Covenant Right Declaration to Healthy Living 27

Chapter 6:
Covenant Right Declaration to Divine Providence 31

Chapter 7:
Covenant Right Declaration to Receiving an Expected End 35

Chapter 8:
Covenant Right Declaration to Liberty From Fears 39

Chapter 9:
Covenant Right Declaration to the Power of God 43

Chapter 10:
Covenant Right Declaration to Be a Carrier of God's Glory 47

Chapter 11:
Covenant Right Declaration to Liberty From Poverty 51

Chapter 12:
Covenant Right Declaration to A Sound Mind 55

Chapter 13:
Covenant Right Declaration to Victory Over Evil Devices 59

Chapter 14:
Covenant Right Declaration to An Evergreen Life 63

Chapter 15:
Covenant Right Declaration to Divine Safety 67

Chapter 16:
Covenant Right Declaration to A Victorious Life 71

Chapter 17:
Covenant Right Declaration to an Excellent Spirit 75

Chapter 18:
Covenant Right Declaration to Total Deliverance 79

Chapter 19:
Covenant Right Declaration to Divine Favour 83

Chapter 20:
Covenant Right Declaration to Divine Immunity Against Collective Affliction 87

Chapter 21:
Covenant Right Declaration to Abundant Life 91

Chapter 22:
Covenant Right Declaration to Reigning In Life 95

Chapter 23:
Covenant Right Declaration to Abundant Grace 99

Chapter 24:
Covenant Right Declaration to Wellness 103

Chapter 25:
Covenant Right Declaration to Safe Delivery 107

Chapter 26:
Covenant Right Declaration to Divine Illumination 111

Chapter 27:
Covenant Right Declaration to Divine Restoration 115

Chapter 28:
Covenant Right Declaration to Live Above Condemnation 119

Chapter 29:
Covenant Right Declaration to Divine Satisfaction 123

Chapter 30:
Covenant Right Declaration to Divine Wisdom 127

Other Books by the Author 131

CHAPTER ONE

COVENANT RIGHT DECLARATION
To Divine Peace

When you are in a difficult situation, and your heart is troubled, remember that God has made provision for your peace in His covenant with you as a believer. God wants you to dwell in peace. In this chapter, you shall declare peace in your life as a child of the covenant through Christ Jesus. It is your covenant right to live peacefully all your days and situations. No power or personality has the right to trouble your peace. May the peace of God abide with you always, in Jesus' name.

> **JOHN 14:27 (KJV):** *Peace I leave with you, my peace I give unto you: not as the world giveth, give I unto you. Let not your heart be troubled, neither let it be afraid.*
>
> **ISAIAH 54:10 (KJV):** *For the mountains shall depart, and the hills be removed; but my kindness shall not depart from thee, neither shall the covenant of my peace be removed, saith the LORD that hath mercy on thee.*

The above Bible verses reveal your right to enjoy unshakable peace and a trouble-free life.

Jesus gave us peace, and the Almighty God made a covenant of peace with us.

This guarantees our right to peace—a life free from trouble and war.

Therefore, when you face any troubling situation, declare your right to divine peace over that situation.

Divine peace is your covenant right, and every creature must respect your right to divine peace as the word of God guarantees it. As a child of the covenant entitled to access and enjoy the peace of God, never settle for a life full of trouble and war. Keep declaring your covenant right to peace over that troubling situation until it obeys your covenant right to peace.

Declare, as follows, your covenant right to divine peace:

I am a child of God's covenant.

According to JOHN 14:27 and ISAIAH 54:10, my covenant right is to enjoy divine peace.

Therefore, I claim my covenant right to divine peace.

I declare the peace of God in and around my life and in my going out and coming in.

I declare the peace of God into my labour and all I put my hands in.

I declare the peace of God into my marriage, work, career, ministry, business, dream, vision, and all that concerns me in Jesus' name.

I declare the peace of God inside my body, soul, and spirit.

I declare that the peace of God shall be around me all my days.

Therefore, I command every war and trouble to cease permanently in all areas of my life.

I command every foundation laid to antagonise peace in my life to be destroyed in Jesus' name.

I command every voice speaking against the peace of God in my life to be permanently silent in Jesus' name.

I command any camp the enemy has set up around my life to oppose the peace of God to be destroyed in Jesus' name.

I command every army of the enemy, waging war against my life in any form, to be removed in Jesus' name.

I command permanent closure on any door opened in my life to hinder peace in Jesus' name.

I command every evil covenant working against peace in my life to be broken in Jesus' name.

I command any evil altar speaking against the peace of God in my life to be destroyed by the fire of God.

I command every arrow of war, targeting my life to backfire.

I command that whoever and whatever will not let me enjoy my covenant right of peace be removed from my way today, in Jesus' name.

I declare that I shall live in peace and have peace all around me in all my days, in Jesus' name.

Covenant-keeping God, I thank you because your covenant of peace has been established around me, and every war has permanently ceased in my life in Jesus' name. Amen.

Additional Bible verses when you need peace.

2 THESSALONIANS 3:16 - *Now the Lord of peace himself give you peace always by all means. The Lord be with you all.*

1 CORINTHIANS 14:33 - *For God is not the author of confusion, but of peace, as in all churches of the saints.*

JOHN 16:33 - *These things I have spoken unto you, that in me ye might have peace. In the world ye shall have tribulation: but be of good cheer; I have overcome the world.*

PHILIPPIANS 4:6 - *Be careful for nothing; but in every thing by prayer and supplication with thanksgiving let your requests be made known unto God.*

ISAIAH 26:3 - *Thou wilt keep him in perfect peace, whose mind is stayed on thee: because he trusteth in thee.*

CHAPTER TWO

COVENANT RIGHT DECLARATION
To A Long Life

God created you to live long and fulfil your destiny. God's plan is that you live to old age and see your children's children. God has made provision for you to live long in His covenant with you as a believer. No power or situation has the right to cut short your life prematurely. When your life is under the threat of death or sickness, you need to arise and declare long-life into your life. You need to refuse to accept that you will die without fulfilling your days. You must declare your covenant right against situations that want to cut short your life. I pray that every terminator assigned against your life will be terminated in Jesus' name.

> **PSALM 118:17 (KJV):** *I shall not die, but live, and declare the works of the LORD.*
>
> **PSALM 91:15-16 (KJV):** *He shall call upon me, and I will answer him: I will be with him in trouble; I will deliver him, and honour him. With long life will I satisfy him, and shew him my salvation.*

The above Bible verses clearly reveal that it is your covenant right to live long and declare the works of the Lord. Almighty God wants you to live long. God created you to live long. God ordained you to live long.

It is your covenant right to live long and not to die young. Therefore, whatever situation wants to cut your life short must be removed. Any situation threatening your life must be defeated. Any incurable sickness that wants to cut short your life must be destroyed. Whatever and whoever that wants to cut short your life must be overthrown. Your covenant right to live long must be respected by any situation or personality.

While it is true that God desires you to live long, it is still your responsibility to claim your covenant right to a long life. If there is any situation threatening your life, you must declare to that situation your covenant right to a long-life.

Declare, as follows, your covenant right to a long-life:

I am a child of God's covenant.

According to PSALM 118:17 and PSALM 91:15-16, it is my covenant right not to die young but to live long.

Therefore, I claim my covenant right to a long life.

I declare that I shall not die but live.

I declare that I shall not die prematurely, and I shall not die before my time. I shall not die suddenly, and I shall not die terribly. I shall not die accidentally, and I shall not die as people of the world die, in Jesus' name.

I declare I shall live long in good health and prosperity in Jesus' name.

I declare that I shall live long to see my children's children, even to the fourth generation, in Jesus' name.

I declare that I shall live long to declare the works of the Lord, in Jesus' name.

Therefore, I command every imagination, expectation, and thought of death to perish out of me from today, in Jesus' name.

I command every voice speaking death into my mind and destiny to be shut down permanently today, in Jesus' name.

I command any evil covenant of death over my life to be broken, in Jesus' name.

I command every arrow of death, targeting me, to backfire, in Jesus' name.

I command any weapon fashioned to cut short my life to fail, in Jesus' name.

I command any altar of death raised against my life to be destroyed by the fire of God, in Jesus' name.

I command any force or personality that wants to cut short my life to be destroyed, in Jesus' name.

I command any demon of death assigned to my life to be bound in Jesus' name.

I command any chain of death designed against my life to be broken in Jesus' name.

I command any situation the enemy has arranged to cut short my life to be scattered, in Jesus' name.

I command the earth to open and swallow any agent of death chasing me in Jesus' name.

I command any mark of premature death on my life to be washed away by the blood of Jesus.

I command any grave dug for me to swallow the owner in Jesus' name.

I shall not die but live in Jesus' name.

Covenant-keeping God, I thank you because your covenant of long life has been established in my life, and I shall live long, and my life shall not be cut short, in Jesus' name.

Additional Bible verses on long life

PROVERBS 3:2 (KJV): *For length of days, and long life, and peace, shall they add to thee.*

ISAIAH 65:20 (KJV): *There shall be no more thence an infant of days, nor an old man that hath not filled his days: for the child shall die an hundred years old; but the sinner being an hundred years old shall be accursed.*

JOB 5:26 (KJV): *Thou shalt come to thy grave in a full age, like as a shock of corn cometh in his season.*

GENESIS 25:8 (KJV): *Then Abraham gave up the ghost, and died in a good old age, an old man, and full of years; and was gathered to his people.*

EXODUS 23:26 (KJV): *There shall nothing cast their young, nor be barren, in thy land: the number of thy days I will fulfil.*

CHAPTER THREE

COVENANT RIGHT DECLARATION
For Stability

When your life becomes unstable and in disorder, you need to remember that God's desire is for your life to be stable and orderly. God has provided stability for your life in His covenant and desires that you live a stable and flourishing life. When you notice that your life is unstable and without direction, you will need to declare your covenant right to a life of stability against that situation making your life unstable. It is my prayer that you will always be unshakable to the enemy in Jesus' name.

> HEBREWS 12:28 (KJV): *Wherefore we receiving a kingdom which cannot be moved, let us have grace, whereby we may serve God acceptably with reverence and godly fear:*
>
> ISAIAH 33:6 (KJV): *And wisdom and knowledge shall be the stability of thy times, and strength of salvation: the fear of the LORD is his treasure.*

The above Bible verses tell us that the kingdom of God is unshakable, and God desires our stability. We are members of a stable and unchanging kingdom under any circumstances.

Therefore, because we belong to an unchanging and always stable kingdom, we have a right to a life of stability. Whatever the circumstances of our lives, God desires that we remain stable and unshaken.

It is your covenant right as a child of the kingdom of God to enjoy a life of stability that any wind of this world can't change.

Declare, as follows, your covenant right to a life of stability under every circumstance of life:

I am a child of God's covenant.

According to HEBREWS 12:28 and NUMBERS 18:19, it is my covenant right to enjoy stability.

Therefore, I claim my covenant right to stability.

I declare stability in and around my life and in all that concerns me.

I declare stability in my career, marriage, business, dream, vision, ministry, work, and everything I put my hands in.

I declare stability in my lifting, enlargement, advancement, progression, and profit-making, in Jesus' name.

I declare stability in my body, soul, and spirit in Jesus' name.

I declare that the situation in and around my life shall always be stable in Jesus' name.

I declare that where God has placed me, I am unshakable, unremovable, untouchable, irreplaceable, indomitable, and unamendable, in Jesus' name.

Therefore, I command any wind that wants to oppose my stability to return to the sender, in Jesus' name.

I command destruction on any foundation laid to destabilise me in any area of life, in Jesus' name.

I command to be sealed up by the blood of Jesus, any opening to instability in my life, in Jesus' name.

I command that any personality (both human and spiritual) that wants to cause instability in any area of my life to receive divine destruction, in Jesus' name.

I command the fire of God to consume to ashes any device and weapon fashioned by the enemy to destabilise me in any form or shape, in Jesus' name.

I command to wither any evil hand stretched into any area of my life to cause instability, in Jesus' name.

I reject instability in my finances, marriage, career, ministry, business, dream, vision, and every other area of my life, in Jesus' name.

I reject for my life emotional instability, psychological instability, spiritual instability, physical instability, mental instability, etc., in Jesus' name.

I shall enjoy divine stability in and around my life in all my days, in Jesus' name.

Covenant-keeping God, I thank you because your covenant of stability has been established around me, and I shall have stability in and around my life. I shall always be unshakable in all my days, in Jesus' name.

Additional Bible verses for stability

PSALM 37:17 (KJV): *For the arms of the wicked shall be broken: but the LORD upholdeth the righteous.*

PROVERBS 3:23 (KJV): *Then shalt thou walk in thy way safely, and thy foot shall not stumble.*

1 SAMUEL 2:9 (KJV): *He will keep the feet of his saints, and the wicked shall be silent in darkness; for by strength shall no man prevail.*

PSALM 62:2 (KJV): *He only is my rock and my salvation; he is my defence; I shall not be greatly moved.*

PSALM 116:8 (KJV): *For thou hast delivered my soul from death, mine eyes from tears, and my feet from falling.*

CHAPTER FOUR

COVENANT RIGHT DECLARATION
To Declare Good Expectations

When your heart is filled with evil expectations and imaginations, you will need to remind yourself that God desires that your expectations and imaginations be good. He desires that you expect something good to happen to you in all situations. It is your covenant right to develop good hope and expectation in all situations, irrespective of how bad the situation may appear on the surface. When you struggle to think and imagine good, it is time to start declaring your covenant right to good expectations. Do not allow the devil to rob you of your blessings and good testimonies by filling your heart with evil expectations and imaginations. You have to fight doubt, fear, and evil imagination with your covenant right to good expectations, as embedded in the word of God. May all your good expectations never be cut short in Jesus' name.

> **PROVERBS 10:28 (KJV):** *The hope of the righteous shall be gladness: but the expectation of the wicked shall perish.*
>
> **ROMANS 5:2 (KJV):** *By whom also we have access by faith into this grace wherein we stand, and rejoice in hope of the glory of God.*

The above Bible verses indicate that, as a believer, you have the right to good expectations. It is your right to expect good things to happen to you.

You have the right to hope for good things because you serve a good God who gives His children good things.

You have the right to expect something good to happen for you, to you, in you, through you, and on your behalf.

When bad things happen to people around you, as a believer, you should expect good things to occur to you. Do not expect bad things to happen to you because bad things are happening to everyone around you. Instead of expecting bad things to come to you, choose to be different and anticipate something good to happen to you. Whatever the situation, it is your right to expect good things because your God is good.

Declare, as follows, your covenant right to good expectations:

I am a child of God's covenant.

According to PROVERBS 10:28 and ROMANS 5:2, it is my covenant right to expect good things to happen to me.

Therefore, I claim my covenant right to good expectations.

I declare that all my expectations will always be good.

I declare that my expectations regarding my career, job, ministry, marriage, and all that concerns me will be good.

I declare that my expectations regarding the work of my hand will be good.

I declare that my expectations regarding my past, present, and future will be good.

I declare that my expectations regarding my future and that of my children, spouse and people connected to me shall be good.

I declare that my expectations regarding my prayer will be good.

I declare that my expectations regarding all my outstanding miracles will be good.

I declare that my expectations regarding all the good seeds I have sown will be good.

I declare that my expectations regarding the treatment I will receive from people will be good.

Therefore, I command every power sending evil expectations into my heart to be broken now, in Jesus' name.

I command every voice speaking evil expectations into my heart to be shut down now, in Jesus' name.

I command any foundation laid for me to expect evil occurrences to be destroyed now, in Jesus' name.

I command whatever in my past, present, and future that wants to make me expect evil to be consumed by the fire of the Holy Ghost, in Jesus' name.

I command the blood of Jesus to separate me from any association sponsoring evil expectations in my heart, in Jesus' name.

I command the blood of Jesus to silence any voice speaking evil expectations into my heart, in Jesus' name.

I command the fire of God to consume any evil sacrifice made by anybody, living or dead, and in any location that is sending evil expectations into my heart, in Jesus' name.

I command any arrow of evil expectations that fires at me to return to the sender, in Jesus' name.

I command permanent shutdown of any accusing voice attacking my heart with guilt and making me expect evil, in Jesus' name.

I command whatever inside of me that is expecting evil to perish now, in Jesus' name.

I reject evil expectations and imaginations concerning my life, in Jesus' name.

I soak my heart and thinking process into the blood of Jesus, and I declare that henceforth, I shall always have good expectations, and my good expectations shall always come to pass, in Jesus' name.

It is my covenant right to expect good things, and I shall always expect good things, in Jesus' name.

Covenant-keeping God, I thank you because your covenant of good expectations has been established in my life and from now on, I shall always have good expectations regarding all that concerns me, in Jesus' name.

Additional Bible verses on good expectations

PSALM 16:9 (KJV): *Therefore my heart is glad, and my glory rejoiceth: my flesh also shall rest in hope.*

2 THESSALONIANS 2:16 (KJV): *Now our Lord Jesus Christ himself, and God, even our Father, which hath loved us, and hath given us everlasting consolation and good hope through grace.*

ROMANS 15:13 (KJV): *Now the God of hope fill you with all joy and peace in believing, that ye may abound in hope, through the power of the Holy Ghost.*

JOEL 3:16 (KJV): *The LORD also shall roar out of Zion, and utter his voice from Jerusalem; and the heavens and the earth shall shake: but the LORD will be the hope of his people, and the strength of the children of Israel.*

PROVERBS 18:10 (KJV): *The name of the LORD is a strong tower: the righteous runneth into it, and is safe.*

CHAPTER FIVE

COVENANT RIGHT DECLARATION
To Healthy Living

God desires a healthy living for you. He wants you to live in good health in all your days. God has incorporated in His covenant your right to a health living. When your health or anything that is yours is under attack, it is time for you to arise and start declaring your covenant right to a healthy living against the situation that wants to make you and what belongs to you sick. Do not permit sickness in any area of your life. It is your covenant right to enjoy a healthy living. I pray that your body systems shall be a no-go area to sickness and disease in Jesus' name.

> 3 JOHN 2 (KJV): *Beloved, I wish above all things that thou mayest prosper and be in health, even as thy soul prospereth.*
>
> ISAIAH 3:10 (KJV): *Say ye to the righteous, that it shall be well with him: for they shall eat the fruit of their doings.*

The above Bible verses reveal that it is in God's plan for you to enjoy healthy living. This is a kind of life whereby you are healthy physically, spiritually, materially, and all round. God wants everything about you to be in good health, whereby nothing is sick in your life.

Declare, as follows, your covenant right to healthy living:

I am a child of God's covenant.

According to 3 JOHN 2 and ISAIAH 3:10, it is my covenant right to enjoy healthy living.

Therefore, I claim my covenant right to healthy living.

I declare a good state of health in every area of my life.

COVENANT RIGHT DECLARATION

I declare that I shall be healthy financially, spiritually, materially, physically, emotionally, psychologically, mentally, maritally, ministerially, career-wise, and in all that concerns me.

I declare good health in my works, visions, dreams, plans, ambitions, desires, and all my pursuits, in Jesus' name.

I declare good health in my going out and coming in, in Jesus' name.

I declare that every good seed I have planted in every area of my life shall be in good health, and none shall die in Jesus' name.

I declare a good state of health in every association in which I will be involved, in Jesus' name.

Therefore, I command any power that wants to make me sick in any area of life to be broken now, in Jesus' name.

I command that any foundation laid for unhealthy living in any area of my life be destroyed, in Jesus' name.

I command any force that wants to corrupt any area of my life to be broken in Jesus' name.

I command any spiritual virus that wants to make any area of my life sick to die by fire, in Jesus' name.

I command any source that wants to send evil flow into any area of my life to dry off, in Jesus' name.

I command death on any seed of sickness planted in any area of my life, in Jesus' name.

I command the blood of Jesus to wash away every mark of sickness in any area of my life in Jesus' name.

It is my covenant right to enjoy healthy living in all areas of my life, and I shall enjoy it all my days, in Jesus' name.

Covenant-keeping God, I thank you because your covenant of healthy living has been established in my life, and from now on, I shall always enjoy healthy living in all areas of my life, in Jesus' name.

Additional Bible verses on healthy living

DEUTERONOMY 7:15 (KJV): *And the LORD will take away from thee all sickness, and will put none of the evil diseases of Egypt, which thou knowest, upon thee; but will lay them upon all them that hate thee.*

ISAIAH 33:24 (KJV): *And the inhabitant shall not say, I am sick: the people that dwell therein shall be forgiven their iniquity.*

PSALM 105:37 (KJV): *He brought them forth also with silver and gold: and there was not one feeble person among their tribes.*

EXODUS 23:25 (KJV): *And ye shall serve the LORD your God, and he shall bless thy bread, and thy water; and I will take sickness away from the midst of thee.*

ISAIAH 58:11 (KJV): *And the LORD shall guide thee continually, and satisfy thy soul in drought, and make fat thy bones: and thou shalt be like a watered garden, and like a spring of water, whose waters fail not.*

CHAPTER SIX

COVENANT RIGHT DECLARATION
To Divine Providence

The Lord wants you to enjoy provisions from Him all your days. He does not want you to live in lack. He has made provision for your needs in His covenant and expects you to take advantage of it whenever you face lack. Do not pass through life like a sheep without a shepherd. When lack threatens you and your plans, start declaring your covenant right to divine providence over the situation. Soon, you will see heaven open over you, and supplies will start flowing in. May you never lack divine providence in all your days, in Jesus' name.

> PSALM 23:1 (KJV): *The LORD is my shepherd; I shall not want.*
>
> PHILIPPIANS 4:19 (KJV): *But my God shall supply all your need according to his riches in glory by Christ Jesus.*

The above Bible verses indicate that God wants to supply all your needs. He wants you to dwell in abundant supplies from heaven. God wants to take care of you in all your days on this earth. Therefore, as a believer, it is your covenant right to enjoy providence from God. It is your covenant right to enjoy care and guidance from the Lord, who saved your life.

Declare, as follows, your covenant right to divine providence:

I am a child of God's covenant.

According to PSALM 23:1 and PHILIPPIANS 4:19, it is my covenant right to enjoy care and provision from the Lord.

Therefore, I claim my covenant right to divine providence.

COVENANT RIGHT DECLARATION

I declare that I shall walk in the care and provision of the Lord in all my days.

I declare that every good thing my life requires shall locate me from the Lord.

I declare that the Lord shall guide my going out and coming in.

I declare that I shall walk under the guidance of God in all ways, in Jesus' name.

I declare that God shall always guide my steps in all my ways, in Jesus' name.

I declare that the Lord will make my way perfect and remove everything that hinders my path, in Jesus' name.

I declare that I shall not want, for the Lord shall be my shepherd, in Jesus' name.

I declare that the eyes of the Lord shall be upon me, leading me right in all my journey, in Jesus' name.

I declare that I shall walk in the strength of the Lord in all my ways, in Jesus' name.

I declare that the Lord shall send his Angels, concerning me in all my ways, in Jesus' name.

I declare divine sustenance into my life in all situations, in Jesus' name.

Therefore, I command any evil hand that wants to lead me away from the care and guidance of the Lord to wither, in Jesus' name.

I command any counsel of the enemy to lead me astray from the Lord's path to come to nought, in Jesus' name.

I command removal and destruction to any blockage of the free flow of divine supplies into my life, in Jesus' name.

I command that whatever will hide my life from divine provision and care is destroyed today, in Jesus' name.

I command that whatever and whoever wants to hinder divine provisions, care, and guidance in my life, to be consumed by the fire of God, in Jesus' name.

I command the rooting out of whatever is planted inside of me that will reject the care and provision of the Lord, in Jesus' name.

I command every mountain that wants to hide me away from the Lord's provision and care to be removed into the sea, in Jesus' name.

I command that whatever in my foundation will frustrate the care of heaven concerning my life be destroyed by fire, in Jesus' name.

I separate myself from every association that will hinder me from constantly enjoying divine providence, in Jesus' name.

It is my covenant right to enjoy divine care and guidance in every area of my life, and I shall enjoy it in all my days, in Jesus' name.

Covenant-keeping God, I thank you because your covenant of divine providence has been established in my life, and from now on, I shall always enjoy the covenant right to divine providence in every area of my life, in Jesus' name.

Additional Bible verses on divine providence

PSALM 84:11 (KJV): *For the LORD God is a sun and shield: the LORD will give grace and glory: no good thing will he withhold from them that walk uprightly.*

PHILIPPIANS 4:19 (KJV): *But my God shall supply all your need according to his riches in glory by Christ Jesus.*

2 CORINTHIANS 9:8 (KJV): *And God is able to make all grace abound toward you; that ye, always having all sufficiency in all things, may abound to every good work.*

PROVERBS 3:10 (KJV): *So shall thy barns be filled with plenty, and thy presses shall burst out with new wine.*

DEUTERONOMY 28:8 (KJV): *The LORD shall command the blessing upon thee in thy storehouses, and in all that thou settest thine hand unto; and he shall bless thee in the land which the LORD thy God giveth thee.*

CHAPTER SEVEN

COVENANT RIGHT DECLARATION
To Receiving an Expected End

Our God never ignores the cries of His children, nor does He ignore making their efforts fruitful. God desires that you don't fail in whatever you pursue. This is God's plan for your life. Whenever it seems as if your expectations are under attack, it is time for you to declare your covenant right to receive your expectations. You must reject failure and whatever wants to frustrate your expectations. I pray that all your plans will come into fulfilment, in Jesus' name.

> JEREMIAH 29:11 (KJV): *For I know the thoughts that I think toward you, saith the LORD, thoughts of peace, and not of evil, to give you an expected end.*
>
> PROVERBS 23:18 (KJV): *For surely there is an end; and thine expectation shall not be cut off.*

The above Bible verses promise that the Lord will grant you your expected end. Your expected end is the final result you wish for—the final outcome you desire concerning your efforts.

In the above Bible verses, God declares His thoughts towards us, which formed part of our covenant right, that He wants to give us an expected end that we desire. Our God is a God of success, not of failure. He wants us to achieve our pursuits.

Declare, as follows, your covenant right to receive an expected end:

I am a child of God's covenant.

According to JEREMIAH 29:11 and PROVERBS 23:18, it is my covenant right to receive my expected end.

COVENANT RIGHT DECLARATION

Therefore, I claim my covenant right to receive my expected end.

I declare a favourable outcome to all my expectations, in Jesus' name.

I declare that I shall achieve every desire of my heart, in Jesus' name.

I declare that all my hopes will be established, in Jesus' name.

I declare that all I desire concerning my career, ministry, marriage, vision, dream, business, and life shall be established in Jesus' name.

I declare that every good seed I sow into my life shall yield favourable fruits, in Jesus' name.

I declare that all my goals and ambitions will be achieved, in Jesus' name.

I declare that every good effort I make towards my life shall bring a bountiful good harvest, in Jesus' name.

I declare that as I aspire to make my life more glorious, the outcome shall be so, in Jesus' name.

Therefore, I command any power that wants to abort my hope to die, in Jesus' name.

I command any evil eye monitoring the result of my good effort for an attack to go blind permanently, in Jesus' name.

I command failure to every machinery fashioned by the enemy against my good effort, in Jesus' name.

I command any evil hand the enemy wants to stretch into my good harvest to wither, in Jesus' name.

Whoever and whatever wants to frustrate my good result shall fail in their mission, in Jesus' name.

I shield all my good harvest with the walls of the fire of God, in Jesus' name.

I command any foundation laid for failure in my life to be destroyed, in Jesus' name.

I command death on any power assigned from hell to frustrate my expected end, in Jesus' name.

I command death on any household enemy that wants to delay or abort the manifestation of my expected end, in Jesus' name.

I decree that my labour over my life shall not be in vain, and all my good expectations shall not fail nor shall they tarry, in Jesus' name.

It is my covenant right to receive my expected end, which I shall receive from the Lord, in Jesus' name.

Covenant-keeping God, I thank you because your covenant of me receiving my expected end has been established in my life and from now on, I shall receive from the Lord all my expected end, in Jesus' name.

Additional Bible verses on receiving your expected ends

ZECHARIAH 4:9 (KJV): *The hands of Zerubbabel have laid the foundation of this house; his hands shall also finish it; and thou shalt know that the LORD of hosts hath sent me unto you.*

PSALM 138:8 (KJV): *The LORD will perfect that which concerneth me: thy mercy, O LORD, endureth for ever: forsake not the works of thine own hands.*

PHILIPPIANS 1:6 (KJV): *Being confident of this very thing, that he which hath begun a good work in you will perform it until the day of Jesus Christ.*

1 THESSALONIANS 5:24 (KJV): *Faithful is he that calleth you, who also will do it.*

2 CHRONICLES 31:21 (KJV): *And in every work that he began in the service of the house of God, and in the law, and in the commandments, to seek his God, he did it with all his heart, and prospered.*

CHAPTER EIGHT

COVENANT RIGHT DECLARATION
To Liberty From Fears

God is a God of love, and there is no fear in love. God desires that you live a life free from every kind of fear. When fear attacks your heart, it is time for you to declare your covenant right against the spirit of fear. Fear is of the devil, and if allowed, it can terminate the glorious destiny God has given you. Do not allow fear to stop you in your destiny, and never should you surrender to fear. When the devil wants to cage you through fear, you must put on resistance against it. It is your covenant right to live above fear. The word of God details your covenant right against fear. I pray that you will live above every manner of fear in all your days, in Jesus' name.

> 2 Timothy 1:7 (KJV): *For God hath not given us the spirit of fear; but of power, and of love, and of a sound mind.*
>
> 2 Corinthians 3:17 (KJV): *Now the Lord is that Spirit: and where the Spirit of the Lord is, there is liberty.*

The above Bible verses state that God has not given us the spirit of fear. This implies that the spirit of fear comes from the enemy. It also means that it is your right to enjoy liberty from every manner of fear. It is part of your covenant right to live free from fear. When fear attacks your mind, declare your covenant right to liberty from fear and send it packing from your life.

Declare, as follows, your covenant right to liberty from fear:

I am a child of God's covenant.

According to 2 TIMOTHY 1:7 and 2 CORINTHIANS 3:17, it is my right to be free from fear and all its attacks.

COVENANT RIGHT DECLARATION

Therefore, I claim my covenant right to liberty from fear.

I declare that I am free from every manner of fears and all their attacks.

I declare that I am free from fear of men, tomorrow, evil occurrences, lack, failure, rejection, sickness, diseases, death, and every other type of fear.

I declare that I am free from every imagination and thought that brings fear, in Jesus' name.

I declare that I am free from every dream, revelation, and prophecy that brings fear, in Jesus' name.

I declare that I am free from fear of pursuing new plans for my life, in Jesus' name.

I declare that I am free from every plan and scheme of the enemy to attack my mind with fear.

I declare that henceforth, I shall not walk in fear, in Jesus' name.

Therefore, I command that every plan of the enemy to stop me with fear be destroyed, in Jesus' name.

I command every seed of fear planted in my mind to die, in Jesus' name.

I command death on whatever in my past, present, or future that is sponsoring fear in my life, in Jesus' name.

I command every word in my heart, making me afraid, to be cancelled, in Jesus' name.

I command any memory that makes me afraid to perish out of me, in Jesus' name.

I command the arrow of fear fired at me to return to the sender, in Jesus' name.

I command death on whatever is in my foundation, sponsoring fear in my life, in Jesus' name.

I command that any structure the enemy has built to sponsor fear in my life to collapse, in Jesus' name.

I command any voice speaking fear into my mind to be shut down permanently, in Jesus' name.

I declare that I will take over any area of my life that fear has conquered from me, in Jesus' name.

I declare that from today, and in all my days, no more fear in my life in Jesus' name.

I shall not be a victim of the attack of the spirit of fear, and my life shall not be dominated by fear, in Jesus' name.

I declare that in all my days, fear shall not stop me, imprison my life, control my destiny, hinder me, keep me stagnant, dominate me, or dictate my plans, in Jesus' name.

It is my covenant right to be free from every kind of fear, and from today, I am free from every kind of fear, in Jesus' name.

Covenant-keeping God, I thank you because your covenant of liberty from fear has been established in my life, and from now on, I shall enjoy liberty from fear, in Jesus' name.

Additional Bible verses on liberty from fear

PROVERBS 28:1 (KJV): *The wicked flee when no man pursueth: but the righteous are bold as a lion.*

ISAIAH 26:3 (KJV): *Thou wilt keep him in perfect peace, whose mind is stayed on thee: because he trusteth in thee.*

PSALM 27:1 (KJV): *A Psalm of David. The LORD is my light and my salvation; whom shall I fear? The LORD is the strength of my life; of whom shall I be afraid?*

HEBREWS 13:6 (KJV): *So that we may boldly say, The Lord is my helper, and I will not fear what man shall do unto me.*

ISAIAH 41:10 (KJV): *Fear thou not; for I am with thee: be not dismayed; for I am thy God: I will strengthen thee; yea, I will help thee; yea, I will uphold thee with the right hand of my righteousness.*

CHAPTER NINE

COVENANT RIGHT DECLARATION
To the Power of God

Power belongs to God, and God desires that we access His power to prevail over every life circumstance. When you feel powerless in life, it is time for you to remember that God has given you His power. When you face stubborn situations, it is time for you to declare God's power over that situation. When you feel weak and powerless, it is time for you to declare God's power over yourself. You can declare God's power over the storm and wind blowing against you. It is your covenant right to access and declare God's power over the situation of your life. May the power of God never leave you, in Jesus' name.

> ACTS 1:8 (KJV): *But ye shall receive power, after that the Holy Ghost is come upon you: and ye shall be witnesses unto me both in Jerusalem, and in all Judaea, and in Samaria, and unto the uttermost part of the earth.*
>
> JOHN 1:12 (KJV): *But as many as received him, to them gave he power to become the sons of God, even to them that believe on his name.*

The above Bible verses state that God has given us power. He has given us the right to access His power. Therefore, it is your covenant right to access and walk in the power of God.

Declare, as follows, your covenant right to access the power of God:

I am a child of God's covenant.

According to ACTS 1:8 and JOHN 1:12, it is my covenant right to access and enjoy the power of God.

COVENANT RIGHT DECLARATION

Therefore, I claim the power of God in every area of my life.

I declare the power of God inside my body, soul, and spirit, in Jesus' name.

I declare the power of God into every system and organ in my body, in Jesus' name.

I declare the power of God into my marriage, finances, career, ministry, work, business, vision, dream, and all that concerns me, in Jesus' name.

I declare the power of God into my life, and all that concerns me, in Jesus' name.

I declare the power of God in and around my home, in Jesus' name.

I declare the power of God into my destiny, engagements, desires, and all my plans, in Jesus' name.

I declare the power of God into my prayer life and every other spiritual activity, in Jesus' name.

I declare the power of God into my going out and coming in, in Jesus' name.

Therefore, I command every negative power at work in any area of my life to be broken in Jesus' name.

I command any negative power from my father's or mother's house, pursuing my life for evil, to be broken, in Jesus' name.

I command any foundation laid for demonic influence on my life to be destroyed, in Jesus' name.

I command any negative power sponsoring evil occurrences in any area of my life to be broken, in Jesus' name.

I command any negative power assigned from hell to make my life miserable, to be broken, in Jesus' name.

I command any negative power assigned against my life to cause destiny failure to be broken, in Jesus' name.

I command any negative power influencing my action to be broken, in Jesus' name.

I command any negative power assigned to frustrate my life to be broken, in Jesus' name.

I command any negative power assigned against my marriage, career, business, ministry, work, vision, dream, and all that concerns me to be broken, in Jesus' name.

I command any negative power that wants to sponsor affliction in my life to be broken, in Jesus' name.

I command any negative power sponsoring any strange event in any area of my life to be broken, in Jesus' name.

I command immediate destruction of whatever will hinder the free flow of God's power into my life, in Jesus' name.

I command every area of my life to come under the dominion of the power of God from now on, in Jesus' name.

I declare that, from today, I am a carrier of God's power, in Jesus' name.

It is my covenant right to access and enjoy God's power, and I shall access and enjoy God's power in all my days, in Jesus' name.

Covenant-keeping God, I thank you because your covenant that gives me the right to access your power has been established in my life, and from now on and in all the days of my life, I shall always access and enjoy your power.

Additional Bible verses on the power of God

ISAIAH 40:29 (KJV): *He giveth power to the faint; and to them that have no might he increaseth strength.*

LUKE 10:19 (KJV): *Behold, I give unto you power to tread on serpents and scorpions, and over all the power of the enemy: and nothing shall by any means hurt you.*

MARK 6:7 (KJV): *And he called unto him the twelve, and began to send them forth by two and two; and gave them power over unclean spirits.*

MICAH 3:8 (KJV): *But truly I am full of power by the spirit of the LORD, and of judgment, and of might, to declare unto Jacob his transgression, and to Israel his sin.*

LUKE 1:35 (KJV): *And the angel answered and said unto her, The Holy Ghost shall come upon thee, and the power of the Highest shall overshadow thee: therefore also that holy thing which shall be born of thee shall be called the Son of God.*

CHAPTER TEN

COVENANT RIGHT DECLARATION
To Be a Carrier of God's Glory

Our God is a God of glory, and He desires that His children carry His glory. God wants you to live a glorious life, not of shame. When shame starts threatening your life, it is time for you to start declaring your covenant right to access the glory of God. When you notice shameful things in any area of your life, it is time for you to declare your covenant right to the glory of God over that situation. As you keep declaring the glory of God over your situation, very soon, you will notice that shame departs as the glory of God starts descending over your life. May the glory of God be evident in your life, in Jesus' name.

> JOHN 17:22 (KJV): *And the glory which thou gavest me I have given them; that they may be one, even as we are one.*
>
> 2 CORINTHIANS 3:18 (KJV): *But we all, with open face beholding as in a glass the glory of the Lord, are changed into the same image from glory to glory, even as by the Spirit of the Lord.*

The above Bible verses indicate that Jesus has given us the glory of God to carry and manifest in our days on earth.

Therefore, it is your covenant right to be the carrier of God's glory as a child of God. The world must see the glory of God in your life. Your life must reflect God's glory, beauty, and honour.

Declare, as follows, your covenant right to be the carrier of God's glory:

I am a child of God's covenant.

According to JOHN 17:22 and 2 CORINTHIANS 3:18, it is my covenant right to carry and enjoy the glory of God.

COVENANT RIGHT DECLARATION

Therefore, I claim my covenant right to carry God's glory.

I declare the glory of God into every area of my life, in Jesus' name.

I declare the glory of God into my marriage, career, business, ministry, finances, work, vision, dream, and all that concerns me, in Jesus' name.

I declare that my entire life is covered with the glory of God.

I declare that my life becomes an advertisement for the glory of God, in Jesus' name.

I declare that whatever I do will be glorious in Jesus' name.

I declare that every event in my life will be glorious, in Jesus' name.

I declare that my performance in all I do will be glorious, in Jesus' name.

I declare that every outcome of my labours will be glorious, in Jesus' name.

I declare that because I carry the glory of God, I become a person of honour, in Jesus' name.

I declare that the world will honour me in all my ways, in Jesus' name.

I declare that every creation shall honour me, in Jesus' name.

I declare that every word of my mouth shall be honoured in Jesus' name.

I declare honour in my going out and coming in, in Jesus' name.

Therefore, I command every foundation of shame to be destroyed in my life, in Jesus' name.

I command any arrow of shame fired at me to return to the sender, in Jesus' name.

I command to be cancelled every mark of shame on my marriage, career, business, ministry, finances, work, vision, dream, and all that concerns me, in Jesus' name.

I command any power that wants to cause me shame to die, in Jesus' name.

I command any spirit of shame to be cast out of my life and come no more, in Jesus' name.

I command immediate favourable turnaround into every event of my life that wants to bring me shame in Jesus' name.

I use the blood of Jesus to separate myself from acquired shame, inherited shame, temporary shame, permanent shame, repeated shame, repairable shame, irreparable shame, inflicted shame, familiar shame, unfamiliar shame, localised shame, general shame, individual shame, collective shame, and any other types of shame, in Jesus' name.

I declare that I am a carrier of God's glory and not a carrier of shame, in Jesus' name.

It is my covenant right to carry the glory of God, and I shall carry the glory of God in all my days, in Jesus' name.

Covenant-keeping God, I thank you because your covenant that gives me the right to be a carrier of your glory has been established in my life, and from today, I shall be carrying the glory of God in all my days.

Additional Bible verses on carrier of God's glory

2 CORINTHIANS 3:18 (KJV): *But we all, with open face beholding as in a glass the glory of the Lord, are changed into the same image from glory to glory, even as by the Spirit of the Lord.*

ROMANS 5:2 (KJV): *By whom also we have access by faith into this grace wherein we stand, and rejoice in hope of the glory of God.*

2 CORINTHIANS 4:6 (KJV): *For God, who commanded the light to shine out of darkness, hath shined in our hearts, to give the light of the knowledge of the glory of God in the face of Jesus Christ.*

JOHN 1:14 (KJV): *And the Word was made flesh, and dwelt among us, (and we beheld his glory, the glory as of the only begotten of the Father,) full of grace and truth.*

PROVERBS 4:18 (KJV): *But the path of the just is as the shining light, that shineth more and more unto the perfect day.*

CHAPTER ELEVEN

COVENANT RIGHT DECLARATION
To Liberty From Poverty

Jesus came to set us free from poverty. God desires His children to access His riches and wealth. God detailed it in His word, your covenant right to be free from poverty and enjoy His riches and wealth. Salvation has set you free from poverty. It is your covenant right to be free from poverty and enjoy the riches and wealth of God. When poverty threatens your life, it is time for you to start declaring your covenant right to be free from poverty. Do not let the devil keep you in poverty. Do not accept that poverty is God's plan for your life. You were saved from the devil to live a life that advertises the riches and wealth of God to the world. May poverty never limit your life, in Jesus' name.

> 2 CORINTHIANS 8:9 (KJV): *For ye know the grace of our Lord Jesus Christ, that, though he was rich, yet for your sakes he became poor, that ye through his poverty might be rich.*
>
> 2 CORINTHIANS 9:8 (KJV): *And God is able to make all grace abound toward you; that ye, always having all sufficiency in all things, may abound to every good work.*

The above Bible verses indicate that Jesus has taken away your poverty and given you His riches. We also see God desiring that we should have all good things in sufficiency.

Therefore, it is your right to be free from any form of poverty. The world defines poverty as a state or condition in which a person or community lacks the financial resources and essentials for a minimum standard of living.

In the kingdom of God, poverty also includes both physical and spiritual lack. The good news is that, as a child of God, Jesus has set you free from any form of poverty.

Declare, as follows, your covenant right to liberty from poverty:

I am a child of God's covenant.

According to 2 CORINTHIANS 8:9 and DEUTERONOMY 15:6, it is my right to be free from poverty.

Therefore, I claim my covenant right to liberty from poverty.

I declare that I am free from any form of poverty, in Jesus' name.

I declare that I am free from absolute poverty (an extreme poverty involving a lack of basic needs). The Lord shall supply all my needs, in Jesus' name.

I declare that I am free from relative poverty (the lack of resources compared to other members of the society). I shall always be numbered among the richest in the land, in Jesus' name.

I declare that I am free from situational poverty (a temporary poverty caused by certain unusual events such as floods or disaster in a nation). I shall live above every situation in the world, as heaven shall be my supplier, in Jesus' name.

I declare that I am free from economic poverty (lack of money to meet my needs). I shall be financially rich and satisfied, in Jesus' name.

I declare that I am free from physical and bodily poverty (lack of access to health facilities). I shall always be in good health, in Jesus' name.

I declare that I am free from mental poverty (lack of access to education and knowledge). I shall always access wisdom, knowledge, and understanding, in Jesus' name.

I declare that I am free from cultural poverty (lack of coming together in a society where the culture does not permit you to join and integrate into the society). I shall not be a castaway, and I shall not be lonely, in Jesus' name.

I declare that I am free from spiritual poverty (lack of understanding of spiritual knowledge and inability to interpret situations spiritually). The spirit of understanding and knowledge shall dwell with me in all my days, in Jesus' name.

I declare that I am free from generational poverty (poverty passed from one generation to another). I disconnect myself from every evil inheritance of poverty, in Jesus' name.

I declare that I am free from secondary poverty (self-inflicted poverty due to wastage that arises from a lack of wisdom to manage resources). I shall always have the wisdom to manage the blessings of the Lord in my life, in Jesus' name.

I declare that I am free from primary poverty (poverty due to a lack of income to meet basic needs, irrespective of level of wisdom). The Lord shall always be my shepherd, and I shall never want, in Jesus' name.

Therefore, every mark of poverty in any area of my life is washed away by the blood of Jesus.

I command any foundation laid for poverty in my life to be destroyed, in Jesus' name.

I command any arrow of poverty fired at me to return to the sender, in Jesus' name.

I declare that in all my days, I shall only lend to nations and never borrow, in Jesus' name.

I declare that the Lord Jesus has taken away my poverty, and He has given me His riches, which shall dwell with me all the days of my life, in Jesus' name.

It is my covenant right to live in liberty from poverty, and I shall always live in this liberty, in Jesus' name.

Covenant-keeping God, I thank you because your covenant that gives me the right to be free from poverty has been established in my life and from today, I shall live in liberty from poverty in all my days.

Additional Bible verses on liberty from poverty

PSALM 35:27 (KJV): *Let them shout for joy, and be glad, that favour my righteous cause: yea, let them say continually, Let the LORD be magnified, which hath pleasure in the prosperity of his servant.*

PROVERBS 8:18 (KJV): *Riches and honour are with me; yea, durable riches and righteousness.*

GENESIS 24:1 (KJV): *And Abraham was old, and well stricken in age: and the LORD had blessed Abraham in all things.*

Deuteronomy 28:12 (KJV): *The LORD shall open unto thee his good treasure, the heaven to give the rain unto thy land in his season, and to bless all the work of thine hand: and thou shalt lend unto many nations, and thou shalt not borrow.*

Proverbs 10:22 (KJV): *The blessing of the LORD, it maketh rich, and he addeth no sorrow with it.*

CHAPTER TWELVE

COVENANT RIGHT DECLARATION
To a Sound Mind

God wants you to live with a sound mind, free from every worry and anxiety of life. A mind fills with the wisdom of God. Therefore, God has included your right to a sound mind in His word of covenant. When your heart is void of wise decisions, it is time to declare to your covenant right to a sound mind. When you face a situation where you don't know what to do next concerning it, and you are confused, then it is time for you to arise and begin to declare to yourself your covenant right to a sound mind. A healthy mind is a gateway to wise decision-making, and it is your right to enjoy a sound mind that will open you to a door of sound judgement with the wisdom of God.

> 2 TIMOTHY 1:7 (KJV): *For God hath not given us the spirit of fear; but of power, and of love, and of a sound mind.*
>
> PROVERBS 2:7 (KJV): *He layeth up sound wisdom for the righteous: he is a buckler to them that walk uprightly.*

The above Bible verses indicate that God has given us sound minds with sound wisdom.

If God has given you a sound mind, it means it is your right to enjoy it.

It is also your right to reject or refuse anything contrary to sound mind.

Declare, as follows, your covenant right to a sound mind:

I am a child of God's covenant.

According to 2 TIMOTHY 1:7, it is my right to enjoy a sound mind.

Therefore, I claim my covenant right to a sound mind.

COVENANT RIGHT DECLARATION

I declare that my mind is sound in the Lord.

I declare that my mind has wise judgement and understanding.

I declare that my mind has self-control and discipline.

I declare that my mind is healthy and stable, in Jesus' name.

I declare that my mind is calm and quiet, in Jesus' name.

I declare that my mind has clarity and discernment, in Jesus' name.

I declare that there is the light of God in my mind, in Jesus' name.

I declare that my mind is balanced and functions under the influence of the Holy Spirit, in Jesus' name.

I declare that my mind is alert and able to see far, in Jesus' name.

I declare that my mind is full of hope and good expectations, in Jesus' name.

Therefore, my mind is free from every worry, anxiety, doubt, fear, uncertainty, torment, agitation, concern, confusion, bitterness, evil imagination, evil thought, and anything that troubles the mind, in Jesus' name.

My mind is free from every attack of depression, oppression, and obsession, in Jesus' name.

My mind is free from any form of irrational thought, in Jesus' name.

I command any attack of the enemy against my mind to be destroyed, in Jesus' name.

I command that any arrow of disturbance the enemy wants to throw at my mind to backfire, in Jesus' name.

I command destruction on whatever is hindering my ability to think godly always, in Jesus' name.

I shall not think evil; I shall not think outside the word of God. I shall not think as the enemy wants me to think. I shall not think worldly. I shall not think carnally. I shall not think as the unbelievers think. I shall not think negatively, but I shall always think as the Spirit-filled child of God, in Jesus' name.

It is my covenant right to enjoy a sound mind, and I shall enjoy a sound mind in all my days, in Jesus' name.

Covenant-keeping God, I thank you because your covenant that gives me the right to enjoy a sound mind has been established in my life, and from today, I shall have a sound mind in all my days.

Additional Bible verses on a sound mind

ISAIAH 11:2-3 (KJV): *And the spirit of the LORD shall rest upon him, the spirit of wisdom and understanding, the spirit of counsel and might, the spirit of knowledge and of the fear of the LORD; And shall make him of quick understanding in the fear of the LORD: and he shall not judge after the sight of his eyes, neither reprove after the hearing of his ears.*

PROVERBS 2:7 (KJV): *He layeth up sound wisdom for the righteous: he is a buckler to them that walk uprightly.*

LUKE 21:15 (KJV): *For I will give you a mouth and wisdom, which all your adversaries shall not be able to gainsay nor resist.*

1 KINGS 3:12 (KJV): *Behold, I have done according to thy words: lo, I have given thee a wise and an understanding heart; so that there was none like thee before thee, neither after thee shall any arise like unto thee.*

DEUTERONOMY 34:9 (KJV): *And Joshua the son of Nun was full of the spirit of wisdom; for Moses had laid his hands upon him: and the children of Israel hearkened unto him, and did as the LORD commanded Moses.*

CHAPTER THIRTEEN

COVENANT RIGHT DECLARATION
To Victory Over Evil Devices

It is God's plan that no weapon fashioned against you should prosper. God wants you to live a life of victory over every device and plan of the wicked. Therefore, God has detailed in His word your covenant right to live a victorious life over the enemy's weapons of warfare. When you face threats of attack, both physical and spiritual, remember that it is your right to be victorious over such plans. Instead of letting fear control you, declare your covenant right over every device the enemy has fashioned against you. Enjoy a life of victory over the enemy's plan and devices, in Jesus' name.

> **ISAIAH 54:17 (KJV):** *No weapon that is formed against thee shall prosper; and every tongue that shall rise against thee in judgment thou shalt condemn. This is the heritage of the servants of the LORD, and their righteousness is of me, saith the LORD.*
>
> **ISAIAH 8:10 (KJV):** *Take counsel together, and it shall come to nought; speak the word, and it shall not stand: for God is with us.*

From the above Bible verses, the word of God tells us that there is no weapon the enemy fashions against us that will prosper.

It implies that it is our covenant right to record victory over every weapon of the enemy.

COVENANT RIGHT DECLARATION

Declare, as follows, your covenant right to victory over evil devices:

I am a child of God's covenant.

According to Isaiah 54:17 and Isaiah 8:10, it is my covenant right to record victory over the enemy's weapon.

Therefore, I claim my covenant right to victory over the enemy's weapons.

I declare that the enemy's weapon of slander and blackmailing shall not prosper against me, in Jesus' name.

I declare that the enemy's weapon of doubt and unbelief shall not prosper against me, in Jesus' name.

I declare that the enemy's weapon of death and destruction shall not prosper against me, in Jesus' name.

I declare that the enemy's weapon of robbery and stealing shall not prosper against me, in Jesus' name.

I declare that the enemy's weapon of hostility and hatred shall not prosper against me, in Jesus' name.

I declare that the enemy's weapon of temptation and sin shall not prosper against me, in Jesus' name.

I declare that the enemy's weapon of persecution and harassment shall not prosper against me, in Jesus' name.

I declare that the enemy's weapon of fear and timidity shall not prosper against me, in Jesus' name.

I declare that the enemy's weapon of rejection and deselection shall not prosper against me, in Jesus' name.

I declare that the enemy's weapon of perversion and manipulation shall not prosper against me, in Jesus' name.

I declare that the enemy's weapon of confusion and indecision shall not prosper against me, in Jesus' name.

I declare that the enemy's weapon of oppression and suppression shall not prosper against me, in Jesus' name.

I declare that the enemy's weapon of ridicule and embarrassment shall not prosper against me, in Jesus' name.

I declare that the enemy's weapon of falsehood and wrong accusation shall not prosper against me, in Jesus' name.

I declare that the enemy's weapon of torture and bullying shall not prosper against me, in Jesus' name.

I declare that the enemy's weapon of divination and incantation shall not prosper against me, in Jesus' name.

I declare that no instrument of war, sword, spear, or arrow (both physical and spiritual) shall prosper against me, in Jesus' name.

I declare that any strife of tongue and word against my life shall fail, in Jesus' name.

Therefore, any effort or plan made against my life, either in the physical or spiritual world, by anybody or personality, or power or individual, or group of individuals, shall fail, in Jesus' name.

Any argument arranged to overthrow the truth in my life shall fail, in Jesus' name.

I shall always walk in justification and vindication against the enemy's attack, in Jesus' name.

In all my days, I shall walk in protection against the enemy's attack and scheme, in Jesus' name.

It is my heritage to walk in victory against every enemy attack, and I shall always walk in victory against the enemy's attacks, in Jesus' name.

Covenant-keeping God, I thank you because your covenant that gives me the right to enjoy victory against the enemy's attack has been established in my life, and from today, I shall always walk in victory against every attack of the enemy, in Jesus' name.

Additional Bible verses on victory over evil devices

JOB 5:12 (KJV): *He disappointeth the devices of the crafty, so that their hands cannot perform their enterprise.*

ISAIAH 54:15 (KJV): *Behold, they shall surely gather together, but not by me: whosoever shall gather together against thee shall fall for thy sake.*

ROMANS 8:1 (KJV): *There is therefore now no condemnation to them which are in Christ Jesus, who walk not after the flesh, but after the Spirit.*

ISAIAH 45:24 (KJV): *Surely, shall one say, in the LORD have I righteousness and strength: even to him shall men come; and all that are incensed against him shall be ashamed.*

JEREMIAH 20:11 (KJV): *But the LORD is with me as a mighty terrible one: therefore my persecutors shall stumble, and they shall not prevail: they shall be greatly ashamed; for they shall not prosper: their everlasting confusion shall never be forgotten.*

CHAPTER FOURTEEN

COVENANT RIGHT DECLARATION
To an Evergreen Life

Our God is evergreen, always fresh and active. God desires His children to be like Him and be evergreen in all their lives. God wants you to always be productive at ages. When you are under the threat of being productive and fruitful, declare your covenant right to a life of evergreen—a life of productivity and fruitfulness without limit. Do not let the devil deceive you to justify an unfruitful life. You were saved to be evergreen and always productive, irrespective of age or life circumstances. Whatever your life situation, believe that you will always be fruitful and productive. I pray that your life will never wither, in Jesus' name.

> **PSALM 1:1-3 (KJV):** *Blessed is the man that walketh not in the counsel of the ungodly, nor standeth in the way of sinners, nor sitteth in the seat of the scornful. But his delight is in the law of the LORD; and in his law doth he meditate day and night. And he shall be like a tree planted by the rivers of water, that bringeth forth his fruit in his season; his leaf also shall not wither; and whatsoever he doeth shall prosper.*
>
> **JEREMIAH 17:8 (KJV):** *For he shall be as a tree planted by the waters, and that spreadeth out her roots by the river, and shall not see when heat cometh, but her leaf shall be green; and shall not be careful in the year of drought, neither shall cease from yielding fruit.*

According to the above Bible verses, it is your right to experience an evergreen life—a perpetually fruitful life irrespective of adverse conditions.

An evergreen life is compared to an evergreen tree—a tree that retains its leaves throughout the year, always bearing fruits and not affected by the change in season.

An evergreen life is a life that is perpetual and always fruitful, and it is never affected by the change in season of life. Such a believer prospers in all things and retains the ability of a fruitful life in all their days and seasons of life.

Declare, as follows, your covenant right to an evergreen life:

I am a child of God's covenant.

According to PSALM 1:1-3 and JEREMIAH 17:8, it is my covenant right to enjoy an evergreen life.

Therefore, I claim my covenant right to an evergreen life.

I declare that I am planted and rooted in the Lord Jesus Christ, my living water.

I declare that I abide in the Lord Jesus all the days of my life.

I declare that my life is well-nourished in the Lord Jesus.

I declare that I lack no good thing in the Lord Jesus Christ.

I declare that my life receives continual grace overflow through the Lord Jesus.

I declare that my life is always fresh and healthy in the Lord Jesus.

I declare that my life bears good fruits always in the Lord Jesus.

I declare that my life is immune against any adverse condition, in Jesus' name.

I declare that my life shall always be fruitful in all seasons of my life, in Jesus' name.

I declare that my life shall always be rich in strength, grace, anointing, and power, in Jesus' name.

I declare that my life shall never wither, in Jesus' name.

I declare that my life shall never depreciate, in Jesus' name.

I declare that my life shall never go backwards, in Jesus' name.

I declare that my life shall never be up and down, in Jesus' name.

I declare that my life shall never fail in prosperity, in Jesus' name.

I declare that every good condition of my life shall never diminish, in Jesus' name.

I declare that the clock of my destiny shall never move backwards, in Jesus' name.

I declare that the sun of my glory shall never go down, in Jesus' name.

I declare that the river of my destiny shall never struggle to flow, in Jesus' name.

I declare that my stars shall never fail to shine, in Jesus' name.

I declare that the light of my destiny shall never go dimmer, in Jesus' name.

I declare that my glory shall never fade away, in Jesus' name.

I declare that my strength shall never abate, in Jesus' name.

I declare that I shall never be an ex-champion, in Jesus' name.

I declare that my life shall retain its divine ordination in all my days, in Jesus' name.

I declare that all seasons shall promote my fruitfulness, in Jesus' name.

Therefore, every attack of the enemy against my perpetual fruitfulness is destroyed, in Jesus' name.

It is my covenant right to enjoy an evergreen life, and I shall enjoy an evergreen life in all my days, in Jesus' name.

Covenant-keeping God, I thank you because your covenant that gives me the right to enjoy an evergreen life has been established in my life and from today, my life shall always be evergreen, in Jesus' name.

Additional Bible verses on evergreen life

ISAIAH 46:4 (KJV): *And even to your old age I am he; and even to hoar hairs will I carry you: I have made, and I will bear; even I will carry, and will deliver you.*

JOB 14:7-9 (KJV): *For there is hope of a tree, if it be cut down, that it will sprout again, and that the tender branch thereof will not cease. Though the root thereof wax old in the earth, and the stock thereof die in the ground; Yet through the scent of water it will bud, and bring forth boughs like a plant.*

GENESIS 49:22 (KJV): *Joseph is a fruitful bough, even a fruitful bough by a well; whose branches run over the wall.*

PSALM 92:13-14 (KJV): *Those that be planted in the house of the LORD shall flourish in the courts of our God. They shall still bring forth fruit in old age; they shall be fat and flourishing.*

JOB 29:19-20 (KJV): *My root was spread out by the waters, and the dew lay all night upon my branch. My glory was fresh in me, and my bow was renewed in my hand.*

CHAPTER FIFTEEN

COVENANT RIGHT DECLARATION
To Divine Safety

God wants your life to be free from every threat of insecurity. He does not want you to live under the threat of the enemy's attack. He has made provision for your safety and incorporated this in His word as a covenant to guarantee your safety in all your days. Therefore, whenever you encounter any threat or insecurity, declare your covenant right to safety over the situation. Refuse to live under insecurity. The Lord is your protector and your keeper. Enjoy a threat-free life in all your days, in Jesus' name.

> **PROVERBS 18:10 (KJV):** *The name of the LORD is a strong tower: the righteous runneth into it, and is safe.*
>
> **ACTS 17:28 (KJV):** *For in him we live, and move, and have our being; as certain also of your own poets have said, for we are also his offspring.*

The above Bible verses declare that safety is found in the Lord, and as believers, we constantly dwell in Him, so we enjoy the right to divine safety.

It is your covenant right to enjoy divine safety with nothing that threatens your security.

Declare, as follows, your covenant right to divine safety:

I am a child of God's covenant.

According to **PROVERB 18:10** and **ACTS 17:28**, it is my covenant right to enjoy divine safety. Therefore, I claim my right to divine safety.

I declare that I am walking in safety, both in the physical and spiritual realms, in Jesus' name.

I declare that I am free from any physical or spiritual attack, in Jesus' name.

I declare that I am free from any form of danger, risk, injury, damage, destruction, accident, harm, hazard, attack, loss, hurt, failure, trouble, and any other adversities, in Jesus' name.

I declare that I am free from any form of demonic attack or attack from the wicked, in Jesus' name.

I declare divine safety into my going out, coming in, when I sleep or awake, and in all my endeavours, in Jesus' name.

I declare that in all my journey, I shall always have a safe arrival, in Jesus' name.

I declare that I shall always walk in victory over any danger, attack, threat, assault, and any evil occurrences, in Jesus' name.

I declare that I am walking in victory over every fear, hunger, lack, sickness, disease, curse, and any device of the wicked, in Jesus' name.

Therefore, whatever and whoever threatens any area of my life shall fail, in Jesus' name.

I command failure to any threat against my life, welfare, fullness of joy, peace, salvation, marriage, career, ministry, job, dream, vision, and anything that concerns me, in Jesus' name.

I command any foundation laid for insecurity in any area of my life to be shattered, in Jesus' name.

I command the total destruction of any structure laid for insecurity in my life, in Jesus' name.

I command that whoever threatens my security shall fall and die suddenly, in Jesus' name.

I command that whoever pursues my life for an evil agenda shall fall and die suddenly, in Jesus' name.

I bind any demon threatening my security, in Jesus' name.

I declare that my way shall be safe, my foot shall not stumble, and I shall not be afraid when I lie down. I shall have no fear of sudden disaster or the ruins that overtake the wicked, for the Lord shall be my safety, in Jesus' name.

To Divine Safety

It is my covenant right to dwell in divine safety, and I shall always dwell in divine safety in all my days, in Jesus' name.

Covenant-keeping God, I thank you because your covenant that gives me the right to enjoy divine safety has been established in my life and from today, I shall enjoy divine safety always, in Jesus' name.

Additional Bible verses on divine safety

ZECHARIAH 2:5 (KJV): *For I, saith the LORD, will be unto her a wall of fire round about, and will be the glory in the midst of her.*

PSALM 91:1-2 (KJV): *He that dwelleth in the secret place of the most High shall abide under the shadow of the Almighty. I will say of the LORD, He is my refuge and my fortress: my God; in him will I trust.*

DEUTERONOMY 33:27 (KJV): *The eternal God is thy refuge, and underneath are the everlasting arms: and he shall thrust out the enemy from before thee; and shall say, Destroy them.*

LUKE 21:18 (KJV): *But there shall not an hair of your head perish.*

JEREMIAH 23:6 (KJV): *In his days Judah shall be saved, and Israel shall dwell safely: and this is his name whereby he shall be called, THE LORD OUR RIGHTEOUSNESS.*

CHAPTER SIXTEEN

COVENANT RIGHT DECLARATION
To A Victorious Life

God hates defeat and does not want His children to live a life of defeat. It is your covenant right to live a life of victory. No matter how strong your enemies may be, your God is stronger than them. Don't lose faith when you face a strong battle from a strong enemy. Instead, declare your covenant right to a victorious life over the situation, and you will see the tide turning in your favour. Do not accept defeat or surrender to a good course. Instead, fight a good fight of faith by declaring your covenant right to a life of victory over the situation. May you never be defeated in life, in Jesus' name.

> 1 CORINTHIANS 15:57 (KJV): *But thanks be to God, which giveth us the victory through our Lord Jesus Christ.*
>
> 2 CORINTHIANS 2:14 (KJV): *Now thanks be unto God, which always causeth us to triumph in Christ, and maketh manifest the savour of his knowledge by us in every place.*

The above Bible verses clearly state that God gives us victory and will always make us walk in victory in all our endeavours.

It implies that God gives us a victorious lifestyle.

It means that it is your right to live a victorious life.

If God gives you a life of victory, it becomes your right to live a life of victory.

Therefore, you must be bold enough to claim a victorious lifestyle—a life that is always winning.

COVENANT RIGHT DECLARATION

Declare, as follows, your covenant right to a victorious life:

I am a child of God's covenant.

According to 1 CORINTHIANS 15:57 and 2 CORINTHIANS 2:14, it is my covenant right to live a victorious life.

Therefore, I claim my covenant right to a victorious life.

I declare my victory over sin, death, grave, fear, intimidation, loss, failure, defeat, stagnancy, poverty, curses, sickness, disease, and every work of Satan, in Jesus' name.

I declare my victory over hell, demons, wicked people, nations, kingdoms, principalities, powers, dominion, and every evil authority, in Jesus' name.

I declare my victory over chariots, chariot riders, evil horses, arrows, and every weapon of warfare of the enemy, in Jesus' name.

I declare my victory over the enemy's plots, wiles, schemes, devices, plans, purpose, games, and every mission of the enemy fashioned against me, in Jesus' name.

I declare my victory over any battles, attacks, oppositions, confrontations, accusations, insinuations, mockery, shame, embarrassment, evil investigation, fault-finding, and every agenda of the enemy to pull me down in Jesus' name.

I declare my victory over evil words, evil thoughts, evil imaginations, evil conclusions, evil expectations, evil prophecies, evil dreams, divination, enchantment, and every demonic utterance assigned against my life in Jesus' name.

I declare my victory over every evil law, decree, oath, arrangement, covenant, agreement, and every evil writing standing against my life, in Jesus' name.

I declare my victory over any evil gang-up, alliance, cooperation, unity, gathering, consultation, and meeting both in the physical and spiritual worlds, in Jesus' name.

I declare my victory over evil altar, prophets, sacrifices, and every demonic activity fashioned against me, in Jesus' name.

I declare my victory over whatever in my past, present, or future that wants to stand against my destiny, in Jesus' name.

The Lord has made me victorious, and I shall live a victorious life.

Therefore, any power, personality, individual, or group of individuals that wants to war against me shall fall for my sake, in Jesus' name.

I command any foundation laid for defeat in my life to be shattered, in Jesus' name.

I command to die by fire, whatever is planted inside of me that attracts defeat, in Jesus' name.

I command the blood of Jesus to separate me from any association, connection, and any factor that will draw me into defeat, in Jesus' name.

It is my covenant right to live a victorious life, and I shall live a victorious life in all my days, in Jesus' name.

Covenant-keeping God, I thank you because your covenant that gives me the right to live a victorious life has been established in my life and from today, I shall live a life of victory in all my days, in Jesus' name.

Additional Bible verses on a victorious life

ROMANS 8:37 (KJV): *Nay, in all these things we are more than conquerors through him that loved us.*

1 JOHN 5:4 (KJV): *For whatsoever is born of God overcometh the world: and this is the victory that overcometh the world, even our faith.*

2 CORINTHIANS 2:14 (KJV): *Now thanks be unto God, which always causeth us to triumph in Christ, and maketh manifest the savour of his knowledge by us in every place.*

JOHN 16:33 (KJV): *These things I have spoken unto you, that in me ye might have peace. In the world ye shall have tribulation: but be of good cheer; I have overcome the world.*

REVELATION 12:11 (KJV): *And they overcame him by the blood of the Lamb, and by the word of their testimony; and they loved not their lives unto the death.*

CHAPTER SEVENTEEN

COVENANT RIGHT DECLARATION
To An Excellent Spirit

Our God is excellent, and His works are always faultless. It is God's desire that His children are also excellent in all that they do. Therefore, God has planted in you an excellent spirit to make you faultless and brilliant in all you do. When you are afraid of laying your hands on new things, remember that you have an excellent spirit dwelling inside of you. When the devil threatens to mess up your work, remind yourself that you carry an excellent spirit. It is your covenant right to operate with an excellent spirit such that your work will always be faultless. You are an intelligent person with the ability to dissolve difficult questions. You have the ability to do well in whatever you do. I pray for you that the excellent spirit inside of you will always be at work in whatever you do, in Jesus' name.

> **DANIEL 6:3 (KJV):** *Then this Daniel was preferred above the presidents and princes, because an excellent spirit was in him; and the king thought to set him over the whole realm.*
>
> **DANIEL 5:12 (KJV):** *Forasmuch as an excellent spirit, and knowledge, and understanding, interpreting of dreams, and shewing of hard sentences, and dissolving of doubts, were found in the same Daniel, whom the king named Belteshazzar: now let Daniel be called, and he will shew the interpretation.*

The above Bible verses reveal that God has given His children excellent spirits to be outstanding and outperform their competitors.

If God has given you an excellent spirit, then it is your right to possess and enjoy the excellent spirit.

Declare, as follows, your covenant right to a victorious life:

I am a child of God's covenant.

According to Daniel 6:3 and Daniel 5:12, it is my covenant right to possess an excellent spirit.

Therefore, I claim my covenant right to an excellent spirit.

I declare that I have an excellent spirit.

I declare that I have intellect and outstanding mental capacity, in Jesus' name.

I declare that I am a person of quick understanding and very knowledgeable, in Jesus' name.

I declare that the spirit of inspiration dwells within me, and I have discernment, in Jesus' name.

I declare that I am diligent, intelligent, brilliant, industrious, skilled, and very smart, in Jesus' name.

I declare that my work is exact, precise, accurate, attractive, admirable, and faultless, in Jesus' name.

I declare that I am exceptional in performance, design, management, planning, and execution of my purpose, in Jesus' name.

I declare that I pay attention to details, operate above error, discover hidden things, and am faultless in all my activities, in Jesus' name.

I declare that my performance is beyond reproach, amendment, adjustment, and any correction, in Jesus' name.

I declare that I am a master and an expert of good work, in Jesus' name.

I declare that I am wonderful and marvellous in action, in Jesus' name.

I declare that I am an asset and a carrier of solutions because the secrets of the Lord dwell with me, in Jesus' name.

I declare that I am superior and anointed above my fellows, in Jesus' name.

I declare that I am a champion that can never be defeated, in Jesus' name.

The Lord has given me an excellent spirit, and I carry an excellent spirit.

Therefore, I bind the spirit of error in my life, in Jesus' name.

I bind the spirit of mediocrity in my life, in Jesus' name.

Any foundation laid for imperfection in my life is destroyed, in Jesus' name.

Any evil eye that wants to fault my work shall be shamed, in Jesus' name.

Any faultfinder assigned against me shall fall for my sake, in Jesus' name.

I declare that none of my competitors shall succeed against me, in Jesus' name.

The Lord has given me an excellent spirit, and I shall operate with excellent spirit in all my days, in Jesus' name.

Covenant-keeping God, I thank you because your covenant that gives me the right to enjoy an excellent spirit has been established in my life, and from today, I shall operate with an excellent spirit in all my days, in Jesus' name.

Additional Bible verses on excellent spirit

JAMES 1:17 (KJV): *Every good gift and every perfect gift is from above, and cometh down from the Father of lights, with whom is no variableness, neither shadow of turning.*

1 SAMUEL 18:14 (KJV): *And David behaved himself wisely in all his ways; and the LORD was with him.*

DANIEL 6:4 (KJV): *Then the presidents and princes sought to find occasion against Daniel concerning the kingdom; but they could find none occasion nor fault; forasmuch as he was faithful, neither was there any error or fault found in him.*

SONG OF SOLOMON 4:7 (KJV): *Thou art all fair, my love; there is no spot in thee.*

PHILIPPIANS 2:15 (KJV): *That ye may be blameless and harmless, the sons of God, without rebuke, in the midst of a crooked and perverse nation, among whom ye shine as lights in the world.*

CHAPTER EIGHTEEN

COVENANT RIGHT DECLARATION
To Total Deliverance

God wants you to enjoy total deliverance—setting free without a left-over of bondage. God wants you to enjoy total liberty so that you can be the person God created you to be. Therefore, it is your covenant right to enjoy total liberty in every area of life. Whenever you notice any restriction in any area of your life, you have to rise and fight it until liberty surfaces. Do not justify limitations or anything that wants to limit you in life. It is your covenant right to be totally free. Enjoy your total freedom in Jesus' name.

> PSALM 34:19 (KJV): *Many are the afflictions of the righteous: but the LORD delivereth him out of them all.*
>
> PSALM 34:6 (KJV): *This poor man cried, and the LORD heard him, and saved him out of all his troubles.*

Total deliverance means freedom from every bondage.

The above Bible verses promise you total deliverance from every bondage.

It implies that it is your right to be delivered from everything that hinders or incapacitates your life.

God does not want you to spend any of your days in the bondage of the enemy.

Declare, as follows, your covenant right to total deliverance:

I am a child of God's covenant.

According to PSALM 34:19 and PSALM 34:6, it is my covenant right to enjoy total deliverance.

COVENANT RIGHT DECLARATION

Therefore, I claim my covenant right to total deliverance.

I declare that every work of Satan in any area of my life is totally destroyed today, in Jesus' name.

I declare that my liberty is perfect, unconditional, unlimited, and unrestricted, in Jesus' name.

I declare that I am totally discharged and acquitted from every accusation of the enemy, in Jesus' name.

I declare that my healing is total, and I have been made whole, in Jesus' name.

I declare that all the prison doors are opened, and I am out of every prison, in Jesus' name.

I declare that I am saved from all troubles and everything that hinders me, in Jesus' name.

I declare that my victory is incontestable and is without reservation, in Jesus' name.

I declare that the Lord Jesus has set me free indeed, and it is irreversible, in Jesus' name.

I declare that my praise is perfect, and my worship is excellent, in Jesus' name.

I declare that my garment of rejoicing is without any stain, in Jesus' name.

I declare that all my pains are gone, and all my bruises are healed, in Jesus' name.

I declare that all my fears are removed, and all my worries are settled, in Jesus' name.

I declare that all my enemies are eliminated and all opposition to my destiny is no more, in Jesus' name.

I declare that I am healed of all sickness and set free from every disease, in Jesus' name.

I declare that all the chains and shackles of the enemy in my life are totally destroyed, in Jesus' name.

I declare that all my infirmities are destroyed, and all my weaknesses are gone, in Jesus' name.

I declare that I am saved from all troubles and preserved from all evil, in Jesus' name.

I declare that there is no left-over of the work of Satan in all areas of my life, for they are totally destroyed, in Jesus' name.

I declare that my victory is total, and my celebration is perfect in Jesus' name.

The Lord has given me total deliverance, and I shall enjoy total deliverance, in Jesus' name.

Therefore, all my oppressors shall die suddenly, in Jesus' name.

I command total destruction to every known and unknown battle in my life, in Jesus' name.

I command total destruction to every power that is sponsoring battle in my life, in Jesus' name.

I command total destruction to everything that incapacitates me in any area of life, in Jesus' name.

I command the rain of fire from heaven, upon all that gathered against me for their total consumption, in Jesus' name.

I am totally delivered, and I shall remain totally free, in Jesus' name.

It is my covenant right to enjoy total deliverance, and I shall enjoy total deliverance in all my days, in Jesus' name.

Covenant-keeping God, I thank you because your covenant that gives me the right to enjoy total deliverance has been established in my life. From today, I shall enjoy total deliverance in all my days, in Jesus' name.

Additional Bible verses on total deliverance

PSALM 34:17 (KJV): *The righteous cry, and the LORD heareth, and delivereth them out of all their troubles.*

JOB 5:19 (KJV): *He shall deliver thee in six troubles: yea, in seven there shall no evil touch thee.*

JEREMIAH 30:7 (KJV): *Alas! For that day is great, so that none is like it: it is even the time of Jacob's trouble; but he shall be saved out of it.*

2 Timothy 3:11 (KJV): *Persecutions, afflictions, which came unto me at Antioch, at Iconium, at Lystra; what persecutions I endured: but out of them all the Lord delivered me.*

2 Corinthians 1:10 (KJV): *Who delivered us from so great a death, and doth deliver: in whom we trust that he will yet deliver us.*

CHAPTER NINETEEN

COVENANT RIGHT DECLARATION
To Divine Favour

God desires that you should enjoy favour because one day of favour can be bigger than many years of hard work. Favour makes life very easy for you and enables you to rise to a greater height with ease and within a short period. The journey of many years can take you a few days with favour. It is your covenant right to enjoy the favour of God. Whenever you want to proceed on anything good, ask God for favour. Furthermore, cultivate the habit of speaking the favour of God into your work and life regularly. Hard work is good, but favour is better. May God's favour work with you in all your days, in Jesus' name.

> **PSALM 5:12** (KJV): *For thou, LORD, wilt bless the righteous; with favour wilt thou compass him as with a shield.*
>
> **PROVERBS 12:2** (KJV): *A good man obtaineth favour of the LORD: but a man of wicked devices will he condemn.*

If God gives you favour such that it encompasses you, it becomes your right to access divine favour. It is your covenant right to enjoy divine favour as a seed of Abraham, a friend of God.

Declare, as follows, your covenant right to total deliverance:

I am a child of God's covenant.

According to **PSALM 5:12** and **PROVERBS 12:2**, it is my covenant right to enjoy favour from God.

Therefore, I claim my covenant right to divine favour.

I declare that I will enjoy divine assistance in all my ways, in Jesus' name.

COVENANT RIGHT DECLARATION

I declare that all the hosts of heaven are walking with me in all my journey, in Jesus' name.

I declare that all creations serve my interest, in Jesus' name.

I declare that my life is daily loaded with benefits by divine provisions, in Jesus' name.

I declare that the face of God shines upon me, and God calls me friend always, in Jesus' name.

I declare that the abundant grace to succeed is upon me in all my endeavours, in Jesus' name.

I declare that heaven has given me all I need to succeed in life, in Jesus' name.

I declare that God is for me, with me, and inside of me, in Jesus' name.

I declare that God is walking with me, walking for me, walking inside of me, and walking through me in all my ways, in Jesus' name.

I declare that I am accepted and embraced by God, in Jesus' name.

I declare that the goodness and mercy of God follow me all days, in Jesus' name.

I declare that God is always generous and kind to me, in Jesus' name.

I declare that I receive good and perfect gifts from the Lord, in Jesus' name.

I declare that the blessing of the Lord is upon me, and I am the blessed of the Lord, in Jesus' name.

I declare that lines are falling for me in pleasant places, and I have a good heritage, in Jesus' name.

I declare that I have unhindered access to heavenly treasures, in Jesus' name.

I declare that God already answers me before I call, in Jesus' name.

I declare that the Lord has made me a strong city, well-fortified by His presence, in Jesus' name.

The Lord has encompassed me with his favour, and I am highly favoured, in Jesus' name.

Therefore, I rebuke every act of rejection in my life from any place, in Jesus' name.

I command destruction to any foundation laid for disfavour in my life, in Jesus' name.

I bind any spirit of disfavour in my life, in Jesus' name.

I command total collapse to any structure supporting hatred in my life, in Jesus' name.

I command total destruction to any power assigned to close the door of favour against me, in Jesus' name.

I command failure to any personality that wants to rob me of my inheritance, in Jesus' name.

The favour of God is with me, and I shall never struggle through life, in Jesus' name.

It is my covenant right to enjoy favour from God, and I shall always enjoy favour from God, in Jesus' name.

Covenant-keeping God, I thank you because your covenant that gives me the right to enjoy divine favour has been established in my life and from today, I shall enjoy divine favour in all my days, in Jesus' name.

Additional Bible verses on divine favour

PSALM 102:13 (KJV): *Thou shalt arise, and have mercy upon Zion: for the time to favour her, yea, the set time, is come.*

EXODUS 12:36 (KJV): *And the LORD gave the people favour in the sight of the Egyptians, so that they lent unto them such things as they required. And they spoiled the Egyptians.*

DEUTERONOMY 33:23 (KJV): *And of Naphtali he said, O Naphtali, satisfied with favour, and full with the blessing of the LORD: possess thou the west and the south.*

1 Samuel 2:26 (KJV): *And the child Samuel grew on, and was in favour both with the LORD, and also with men.*

Proverbs 12:2 (KJV): *A good man obtaineth favour of the LORD: but a man of wicked devices will he condemn.*

CHAPTER TWENTY

COVENANT RIGHT DECLARATION
To Divine Immunity Against Collective Affliction

God has given you immunity against any affliction that will befall the world. God desires that you enjoy an exception from every evil the world will encounter. It is your covenant right not to partake in any evil that will befall the world. When you hear that evil is coming to the world, declare your covenant right to immunity against such affliction. When you notice evil befalling people around you, separate yourself by declaring your immunity against affliction. Do not expect the evil that befalls the world to come to you, but rather, separate yourself from it by standing on the word of covenant written by God. You shall not partake in collective affliction in Jesus' name.

> **PSALM 91:7-8 (KJV):** *A thousand shall fall at thy side, and ten thousand at thy right hand; but it shall not come nigh thee. Only with thine eyes shalt thou behold and see the reward of the wicked.*
>
> **EXODUS 8:22-23 (KJV):** *And I will sever in that day the land of Goshen, in which my people dwell, that no swarms of flies shall be there; to the end thou mayest know that I am the LORD in the midst of the earth. And I will put a division between my people and thy people: to morrow shall this sign be.*

The above Bible verses promise that you shall not partake in general affliction that befalls the world. The evil that befalls the world shall not come near you.

This implies your right to refuse and reject anything that wants to draw you into general or common affliction. You have the right to immunity against collective affliction.

Declare, as follows, your covenant right to divine immunity against collective affliction:

I am a child of God's covenant.

According to PSALM 91:7-8 and EXODUS 8:22-23, it is my covenant right to enjoy divine immunity against collective affliction.

Therefore, I claim my covenant right to divine immunity against collective affliction.

I declare that I have divine immunity against any infectious disease, whether general or localised.

I declare that I have been forgiven of any sin or wrongdoing capable of making me partake in collective affliction.

I declare that I have been exonerated from any judgment and accusation to partake in any collective affliction.

I declare that I am not condemned with the world to suffer affliction, in Jesus' name.

I declare that my name is not in the book of those to suffer affliction in the world, in Jesus' name.

I declare that I am the object of the Lord's distinguished care, in Jesus' name.

I declare that the Lord has made me the candidate of His perfect protection against every danger and trouble, in Jesus' name.

I declare that the tender mercy of God guarantees my utmost protection against every evil in Jesus' name.

I declare that I am not a victim of a common calamity or any epidemic, in Jesus' name.

I declare that I am preserved against general destruction and every manner of danger, in Jesus' name.

I declare that the Lord has given me a special exemption, which secures my safety amid dangers.

I declare that I have divine immunity against any general calamity, illness, disease, infirmity, pain, sorrow, misery, plague, misfortune, grief, torment, adversity, distress, trial, tribulation, suffering, and any other difficulties, in Jesus' name.

I declare that I am saved, secured, and protected from everything that troubles the world, in Jesus' name. I am safe at all times, both in the day and night, in Jesus' name.

I declare that I am immune against devouring pestilence, fatal pestilence, the pestilence that distributes sickness and death, pestilence of the wicked, pestilence of divine judgement, pestilence of contagious diseases, the pestilence that walks in the day and night, the pestilence that causes diverse destruction, and every pestilence that endangers and threatens the welfare of the people.

Therefore, every association, link, or connection between me and the world that will draw me into general affliction is broken today, in Jesus' name.

I command any power that wants to connect me to the evil that befalls the world to be broken, in Jesus' name.

I command to die any personality that wants to make me the victim of common affliction, in Jesus' name.

I command to die anything in my foundation that will make me a victim of common affliction, in Jesus' name.

The Lord has given me divine immunity against general affliction, and I shall never partake in general affliction, in Jesus' name.

Covenant-keeping God, I thank you because your covenant that gives me immunity against collective affliction has been established in my life, and from today, I shall enjoy divine immunity against collective affliction in all my days, in Jesus' name.

Additional Bible verses on divine immunity against collective affliction

MALACHI 3:18 (KJV): *Then shall ye return, and discern between the righteous and the wicked, between him that serveth God and him that serveth him not.*

PSALM 32:6 (KJV): *For this shall every one that is godly pray unto thee in a time when thou mayest be found: surely in the floods of great waters they shall not come nigh unto him.*

Exodus 12:13 (KJV): *And the blood shall be to you for a token upon the houses where ye are: and when I see the blood, I will pass over you, and the plague shall not be upon you to destroy you, when I smite the land of Egypt.*

Psalm 121:6-8 (KJV): *The sun shall not smite thee by day, nor the moon by night. The LORD shall preserve thee from all evil: he shall preserve thy soul. The LORD shall preserve thy going out and thy coming in from this time forth, and even for evermore.*

2 Peter 2:9 (KJV): *The Lord knoweth how to deliver the godly out of temptations, and to reserve the unjust unto the day of judgment to be punished.*

CHAPTER TWENTY-ONE

COVENANT RIGHT DECLARATION
To Abundant Life

Our God is the God of abundance who has all good things beyond measure. He desires that your life be an expression of His unlimited blessings. It is your covenant right to live a life filled with abundance of every good thing from the Lord. The abundant life Jesus brought us guarantees overflowing blessings from the Lord and a life without limit. When life brings limitations in your way, declare your covenant right to an abundant life over that situation, and you will see the tide change in your favour. I pray for you that you will live a life of abundant blessings from the Lord, in Jesus' name.

> **JOHN 10:10 (KJV):** *The thief cometh not, but for to steal, and to kill, and to destroy: I am come that they might have life, and that they might have it more abundantly.*
>
> **2 CORINTHIANS 9:8 (KJV):** *And God is able to make all grace abound toward you; that ye, always having all sufficiency in all things, may abound to every good work.*

According to the above Bible verses, Jesus has given us abundant life to enjoy, and it is our right to enjoy it. Also, it is your responsibility to claim it; after all, the Lord has given it to you.

Declare, as follows, your covenant right to abundant life:

I am a child of God's covenant.

According to John 10:10 and 2 Corinthians 9:8, it is my covenant right to enjoy an abundant life because the Lord has given me abundant life to enjoy.

Therefore, I claim my covenant right to abundant life.

I declare that the abundant grace of God is upon my life, in Jesus' name.

I declare that I have abundant grace to make wealth and riches in great measure in Jesus' name.

I declare that I am blessed spiritually, physically, and economically, in Jesus' name.

I declare that I have physical and material prosperity with good health and well-being, in Jesus' name.

I declare that I possess, without measure, all the good things of life, in Jesus' name.

I declare that my coast is enlarged, and my dominion is beyond the enemy's limitations.

I declare that I have life in its abounding fullness of joy, peace, love, and strength for mind, body, and soul, in Jesus' name.

I declare that the blessing of the Lord in my life is exceedingly great and beyond my expectations, in Jesus' name.

I declare that the blessings of the Lord upon my life are plenteous and more than sufficient, in Jesus' name.

I declare that my life is rich in divine provisions, in Jesus' name.

I declare that I have an unlimited and superabundant supply of good things from the Lord, in Jesus' name.

I declare that the blessings of the Lord in my life are uncountable and beyond measure, in Jesus' name.

I declare that my cup runs over with the blessings of the Lord, in Jesus' name.

I declare that my house is full of the blessings of the Lord, in Jesus' name.

I declare that I have overflowing blessings with more than enough to eat, in Jesus' name.

The Lord has given me abundant life, and it is my right to enjoy it.

Therefore, every limitation and boundary the enemy has placed upon my life is broken today, in Jesus' name.

Any ceiling the enemy has placed over my life is broken today, in Jesus' name.

Any foundation laid for a life of limitation is broken in my life, in Jesus' name.

Any demonic regulation and control placed over my life is destroyed, in Jesus' name.

I break any mark of scarcity and insufficiency of good things in my life, in Jesus' name.

I shall not lack good things, in Jesus' name.

The abundant blessing of the Lord in my life is never-ending, ceaseless, continuous, constant, inexhaustible (never gets finished), unbroken, timeless, nonstop, perpetual, and it is a lifetime, in Jesus' name.

It is my covenant right to enjoy abundant life, and I shall always enjoy abundant life in all my days, in Jesus' name.

Covenant-keeping God, I thank you because your covenant that gives me abundant life has been established in my life, and from today, I shall enjoy abundant life in all my days, in Jesus' name.

Additional Bible verses on abundant life

EPHESIANS 3:20 (KJV): *Now unto him that is able to do exceeding abundantly above all that we ask or think, according to the power that worketh in us.*

PSALM 103:5 (KJV): *Who satisfieth thy mouth with good things; so that thy youth is renewed like the eagle's.*

2 PETER 1:11 (KJV): *For so an entrance shall be ministered unto you abundantly into the everlasting kingdom of our Lord and Saviour Jesus Christ.*

PSALM 16:11 (KJV): *Thou wilt shew me the path of life: in thy presence is fulness of joy; at thy right hand there are pleasures for evermore.*

PSALM 23:5 (KJV): *Thou preparest a table before me in the presence of mine enemies: thou anointest my head with oil; my cup runneth over.*

CHAPTER TWENTY-TWO

COVENANT RIGHT DECLARATION
To Reigning in Life

Our God is the King of all kings and has also made us kings. Our God reigns over all things, so He made us reign over all things. It is your covenant right to live a life of dominion as a king. You were saved to reign over all things, both good and bad. When life wants to dominate you, it is time for you to declare your covenant right to reign in life over that situation. Do not let life rule over you, but rule over life. You are a king installed by the Lord to reign in life. May you reign in life, in Jesus' name.

> ROMANS 5:17 (KJV): *For if by one man's offence death reigned by one; much more they which receive abundance of grace and of the gift of righteousness shall reign in life by one, Jesus Christ.*
>
> REVELATION 1:6 (KJV): *And hath made us kings and priests unto God and his Father; to him be glory and dominion for ever and ever. Amen.*

The above Bible verses confirm that you have been made to reign in life through the grace and gift of righteousness from the Lord Jesus Christ.

Therefore, it is your right to reign in life.

Declare, as follows, your covenant right to reign in life:

I am a child of God's covenant.

According to ROMANS 5:17 and ROMANS 1:6, it is my covenant right to reign in life.

Therefore, I claim my covenant right to reign in life.

I declare that the Lord Jesus has given me the fullness of grace and the gift of righteousness to reign in life.

COVENANT RIGHT DECLARATION

I declare that the Lord Jesus has made me king and priest unto God in His name.

I declare I am a king with dominion to reign in life, in Jesus' name.

I declare that I occupy a secure and exalted position in the heavenlies with the Lord Jesus Christ.

I declare that through the Lord Jesus Christ, I have overcome all my physical and spiritual enemies, in Jesus' name.

I declare that all my enemies are now under my feet, and they will never rise against me anymore, in Jesus' name.

I declare that through the Lord Jesus Christ, I reign over Satan and his cohorts, the world, difficulties, temptation, fear, death, defeat, depression, poverty, curses, sickness, diseases, adverse surroundings and every circumstance of life, in Jesus' name.

I declare that through the Lord Jesus Christ, I reign over wealth, riches, prosperity, and every blessing from the Lord, in Jesus' name.

I declare that at my command, every evil shall bow before me and obey my voice, in Jesus' name.

I declare that at my command, every good thing from the Lord comes unto me, in Jesus' name.

I declare that I have control and direct influence over life and all that concerns me, in Jesus' name.

I declare that in every situation and circumstance of life, obey my command, in Jesus' name.

I declare that through the Lord Jesus, I am more than a conqueror.

I declare that my territory is peaceful, and all my jurisdiction is secured, in Jesus' name.

I declare that I dominate, dictate, control, govern, and order every event of my life as it pleases me, in Jesus' name.

I declare that every authority and establishment shall serve my purpose, in Jesus' name.

The Lord Jesus has given me grace and righteousness to reign in life, and I shall reign in life in all my days.

Therefore, every evil dominion in any area of my life is removed today, in Jesus' name.

Every evil power exercising authority over any area of my life is broken, in Jesus' name.

Whatever is contrary to God that has been reigning in any area of my life is destroyed today, in Jesus' name.

Every reign of terror, threat, and fear in any area of my life is today cancelled, in Jesus' name.

Every tyrant who occupies a position of authority in any area of my life is today brought into destruction, in Jesus' name.

Any power challenging my dominion is today broken into pieces, in Jesus' name.

It is my covenant right to reign in life, and I shall reign in life in all my days, in Jesus' name.

Covenant-keeping God, I thank you because your covenant that gives me the right to reign in life has been established in my life and from today. I shall reign in life in all my days, in Jesus' name.

Additional Bible verses on reigning in life

GENESIS 1:28 (KJV): *And God blessed them, and God said unto them, Be fruitful, and multiply, and replenish the earth, and subdue it: and have dominion over the fish of the sea, and over the fowl of the air, and over every living thing that moveth upon the earth.*

1 CORINTHIANS 4:8 (KJV): *Now ye are full, now ye are rich, ye have reigned as kings without us: and I would to God ye did reign, that we also might reign with you.*

1 PETER 2:9 (KJV): *But ye are a chosen generation, a royal priesthood, an holy nation, a peculiar people; that ye should shew forth the praises of him who hath called you out of darkness into his marvellous light.*

PSALM 8:6 (KJV): *Thou madest him to have dominion over the works of thy hands; thou hast put all things under his feet.*

2 PETER 1:3 (KJV): *According as his divine power hath given unto us all things that pertain unto life and godliness, through the knowledge of him that hath called us to glory and virtue.*

CHAPTER TWENTY-THREE

COVENANT RIGHT DECLARATION
To Abundant Grace

God gives us grace to enable us to do what is beyond our natural ability. With the grace of God at work in your life, you can do greater things and climb to a height far beyond your reach with your natural ability. This grace of God is abundant in your life, and this is to make it easy for you to perform beyond your natural ability in every facet of life. The abundant grace of God on your life makes you unstoppable in all life situations. It is your covenant right to declare your right to the abundant grace of God whenever you face tasks that appear difficult and impossible. May your life become a testimony to the wonder-working power of the abundant grace of God, in Jesus' name.

> 2 CORINTHIANS 9:8 (KJV): *And God is able to make all grace abound toward you; that ye, always having all sufficiency in all things, may abound to every good work:*
>
> 2 CORINTHIANS 4:15 (KJV): *For all things are for your sakes, that the abundant grace might through the thanksgiving of many redound to the glory of God.*

Grace is the unmerited favour God bestows on His children. This grace enables us to perform beyond our natural abilities.

The above Bible verses reveal that the Lord has bestowed on us abundant grace. Therefore, it is your covenant right to enjoy abundant grace from the Lord.

Declare, as follows, your covenant right to abundant grace:

I am a child of God's covenant.

According to 2 CORINTHIANS 9:8 and 2 CORINTHIANS 4:15, it is my covenant right to access and enjoy abundant grace from the Lord.

Therefore, I claim my covenant right to abundant grace.

I declare that I have abundant grace of favour and mercy from the Lord, in Jesus' name.

I declare that the grace of God has made me a partaker of the diverse blessings of the Lord, in Jesus' name.

I declare that I have justifying grace from the Lord. The Lord Jesus has made me qualified to access divine grace.

I declare that I have sanctifying grace from the Lord. The Lord Jesus has made me holy to access divine grace.

I declare that I have glorifying grace from the Lord. The Lord Jesus has glorified me with divine grace.

I declare that God's abundant grace has made me stronger than any challenge, obstacle, hatred, difficulty, attack, opposition, and anything that hinders, in Jesus' name.

I declare that I advance in grace as the Lord Jesus moves me from grace to grace, giving me more and more grace.

I declare that I have abundant grace to do the impossible and complete all that I lay my hands on, in Jesus' name.

I declare that I have abundant grace to defeat all evils, in Jesus' name.

I declare that I have abundant grace to be unstoppable, unconquerable, uncontainable, undefeatable, irrepressible, unrestrainable, unquenchable, and unbreakable, in Jesus' name.

I declare that I have abundant grace to go from strength to strength, power to power, victory to victory, success to success, and progress to progress in all my days in Jesus' name.

I declare that I have abundant grace never to quit or give up a good fight, in Jesus' name.

I declare that I have abundant grace to meet all my needs and possess all the resources to complete all my tasks, in Jesus' name.

I declare that I have abundant grace to hear the inaudible and access the secret things of the Lord, in Jesus' name.

I declare that I have abundant grace to excel in all my tasks, in Jesus' name.

I declare that I have abundant grace to rise with ease and have a comfortable ride through life, in Jesus' name.

I declare that I have abundant grace to always win in life, in Jesus' name.

I declare that I have abundant grace to run my race without getting weary and faint, in Jesus' name.

I declare that the abundant grace of God has given me divine favour, human favour, governmental favour, angelic favour, covenant-based favour, general favour, random favour, collective favour, generational favour, direct favour, indirect favour, progressive favour, all-round favour, and favour of a lifetime, in Jesus' name.

The Lord Jesus has given me abundant grace to enjoy for life, and I shall access and enjoy the abundant grace from the Lord in all my days, in Jesus' name.

Covenant-keeping God, I thank you because your covenant that gives me the right to enjoy your abundant grace has been established in my life, and from today, I shall enjoy your abundant grace in all my days, in Jesus' name.

Additional Bible Verses On Abundant Grace

PHILIPPIANS 4:13 (KJV): *I can do all things through Christ which strengtheneth me.*

2 CORINTHIANS 3:5 (KJV): *Not that we are sufficient of ourselves to think any thing as of ourselves; but our sufficiency is of God.*

1 CHRONICLES 29:12 (KJV): *Both riches and honour come of thee, and thou reignest over all; and in thine hand is power and might; and in thine hand it is to make great, and to give strength unto all.*

Hebrews 13:21 (KJV): *Make you perfect in every good work to do his will, working in you that which is wellpleasing in his sight, through Jesus Christ; to whom be glory for ever and ever. Amen.*

Joshua 17:13 (KJV): *Yet it came to pass, when the children of Israel were waxen strong, that they put the Canaanites to tribute; but did not utterly drive them out.*

CHAPTER TWENTY-FOUR

COVENANT RIGHT DECLARATION
To Wellness

God wants all things to be well with you such that in all things, you shall suffer no sickness. God wants it to be well with you in every situation you may find yourself in. He wants it to be well with you financially, ministerially, maritally, etc. Therefore, you have a covenant right to enjoy wellness in all things. When it seems as if things are not going well with you in any area of life, it is time for you to begin to declare your covenant right to wellness. Declare your covenant right to wellness over your marriage, business, career, and other areas of your life that are not performing well. As you declare your covenant right to wellness by faith, you will begin to discover wellness in every area of your life. I pray it will always be well with you, in Jesus' name.

> ISAIAH 3:10 (KJV): *Say ye to the righteous, that it shall be well with him: for they shall eat the fruit of their doings.*
>
> JEREMIAH 15:11 (KJV): *The LORD said, Verily it shall be well with thy remnant; verily I will cause the enemy to entreat thee well in the time of evil and in the time of affliction.*

The above Bible verses show that God has given you a gift of wellness. Therefore, it is your covenant right to enjoy wellness.

Declare, as follows, your covenant right to wellness:

I am a child of God's covenant.

According to ISAIAH 3:10 and JEREMIAH 15:11, it is my covenant right to enjoy wellness.

Therefore, I claim my covenant right to wellness.

COVENANT RIGHT DECLARATION

I declare that God's abundant grace has given me the gift of righteousness. Therefore, I have the righteousness of the Lord Jesus Christ.

I declare that I have a reward of happiness for all my labour, in Jesus' name.

I declare that I shall eat the fruits of all my labours, in Jesus' name.

I declare that it shall be well with me in every situation and condition of life, in Jesus' name.

I declare that it shall be well with me in every period, stage, and phase of life, in Jesus' name.

I declare it shall be well with me in all I do, in Jesus' name.

I declare that it shall be well with me in my going out and coming in, in Jesus' name.

I declare that I have wellness in all dimensions of life, in Jesus' name.

I declare that I have spiritual wellness. I am spiritually healthy and strongly connected to my creator, in Jesus' name.

I declare I have emotional wellness—I am emotionally stable and balanced, in Jesus' name.

I declare that I have occupational wellness. I have career satisfaction with many opportunities coming to me, in Jesus' name.

I declare that I have intellectual wellness. I am creative and extremely intelligent, in Jesus' name.

I declare that I have financial wellness. I am a good manager of my finances, and I lend to nations, in Jesus' name.

I declare that I have physical wellness. I am generally healthy and strong with habits and behaviours that promote good health in me, in Jesus' name.

I declare that I have environmental wellness. I have a good relationship with my community (environment and people around me). I am blessed by my environment, in Jesus' name.

I declare that I have social wellness. I am of meaningful and supportive interaction and engagement with communities, groups, and people around me without conflict of interest or clashes of culture. I have peace with people around me, in Jesus' name.

The Lord has given me wellness as a gift, and I shall enjoy it all my days, in Jesus' name.

Therefore, whatever that wants to trouble my well-being shall perish, in Jesus' name.

It is my covenant right to enjoy wellness, and I shall enjoy wellness in all my days, in Jesus' name.

Covenant-keeping God, I thank you because your covenant that gives me the right to enjoy wellness has been established in my life and from today, I shall enjoy wellness in every dimension of life in all my days, in Jesus' name.

Additional Bible verses on wellness

HOSEA 14:5-6 (KJV): *I will be as the dew unto Israel: he shall grow as the lily, and cast forth his roots as Lebanon. His branches shall spread, and his beauty shall be as the olive tree, and his smell as Lebanon.*

JEREMIAH 33:6 (KJV): *Behold, I will bring it health and cure, and I will cure them, and will reveal unto them the abundance of peace and truth.*

PSALM 72:7 (KJV): *In his days shall the righteous flourish; and abundance of peace so long as the moon endureth.*

MALACHI 4:2 (KJV): *But unto you that fear my name shall the Sun of righteousness arise with healing in his wings; and ye shall go forth, and grow up as calves of the stall.*

ISAIAH 53:5 (KJV): *But he was wounded for our transgressions, he was bruised for our iniquities: the chastisement of our peace was upon him; and with his stripes we are healed.*

CHAPTER TWENTY-FIVE

COVENANT RIGHT DECLARATION
To Safe Delivery

It is to the glory of God that whenever He enables you to conceive an idea, you are able to deliver it safely and bring it to fruition. God wants you to have a safe delivery of every dream and vision He enables you to conceive. When your plan comes under attack, it is time for you to declare your covenant right to safe delivery over the situation. When it seems as if your dream will be aborted, instead of accepting defeat, declare your covenant right to safe delivery over the situation. No enemy can abort your good plan unless you give up or quit. It is your covenant right to conceive, carry, and deliver safely every good idea and plan. May your plan never be aborted, in Jesus' name.

> **EXODUS 23:26 (KJV):** *There shall nothing cast their young, nor be barren, in thy land: the number of thy days I will fulfil.*
>
> **PSALM 107:38 (KJV):** *He blesseth them also, so that they are multiplied greatly; and suffereth not their cattle to decrease.*

The above Bible verses give a promise to children of God that when they conceive, they shall deliver safely. We all have in us a part that functions like a womb, where good ideas are planted and nurtured until the time of bringing them forth into physical existence comes. It is in the plan of God that whatever good thing God enables you to conceive, there shall be safe delivery.

Therefore, it is your covenant right to experience the safe delivery of every good thing God enables you to conceive.

Declare, as follows, your covenant right to safe delivery:

I am a child of God's covenant.

According to Exodus 23:26 and Psalm 107:38, it is my covenant right to safely deliver every good thing I conceive.

Therefore, I claim my covenant right to the safe delivery of good things.

I declare that the grace of God is upon me to conceive, carry, and deliver safely every blessing from God, in Jesus' name.

I declare that the Lord has given me strength both to conceive and to retain the conception of blessings from the Lord till the natural and proper time of bringing forth, in Jesus' name.

I declare that I shall safely deliver my conceived dream, vision, plans, purpose, ideas, pursuit, ambition, expectations, hope, and every blessing God planted in me, in Jesus' name.

I declare concerning every blessing I conceive that the delivery shall be timely, perfect, easy, comfortable, natural, sweet, excellent, peaceful, joyous, exciting, healthy, stress-free, and without any complication, in Jesus' name.

I declare safe arrival to every one of my expected blessings, in Jesus' name.

It is my covenant right to have the safe delivery of every one of my conceived blessings.

Therefore, I declare I shall not labour in vain, in Jesus' name.

I command to be removed from my way of delivering blessing, any obstruction, ungodly delay, hindrance, attack, danger, threat, anguish, pain, opposition, restraint, distress, complication, challenge, and any force that frustrates safe delivery, in Jesus' name.

I command to go blind, any evil eye monitoring the day of delivery of my blessings, in Jesus' name.

I command any evil hand waiting to cause the stillbirth of my conceived blessings to wither, in Jesus' name.

I command any demonic arrangement against the safe delivery of my conceived blessings to scatter, in Jesus' name.

I command the breakage of any power assigned to retain or restrain the delivery of my blessings, in Jesus' name.

There shall be no abortion or miscarriage of any of my conceived blessings, in Jesus' name.

It is my covenant right to have a safe delivery of every conceived blessings, and I shall always have a safe delivery of all my conceived blessings, in Jesus' name.

Covenant-keeping God, I thank you because your covenant that gives me the right to a safe delivery of every one of my conceived blessings has been established in my life, and from today on, I shall always have a safe delivery of every blessing I conceive, in Jesus' name.

Additional Bible verses on safe delivery

PROVERBS 16:3 (KJV): *Commit thy works unto the LORD, and thy thoughts shall be established.*

PSALM 144:13-14 (KJV): *That our garners may be full, affording all manner of store: that our sheep may bring forth thousands and ten thousands in our streets: That our oxen may be strong to labour; that there be no breaking in, nor going out; that there be no complaining in our streets.*

ISAIAH 66:9 (KJV): *Shall I bring to the birth, and not cause to bring forth? saith the LORD: shall I cause to bring forth, and shut the womb? saith thy God.*

PSALM 107:38 (KJV): *He blesseth them also, so that they are multiplied greatly; and suffereth not their cattle to decrease.*

PSALM 90:17 (KJV): *And let the beauty of the LORD our God be upon us: and establish thou the work of our hands upon us; yea, the work of our hands establish thou it.*

CHAPTER TWENTY-SIX

COVENANT RIGHT DECLARATION
To Divine Illumination

God is light, and in Him there is no darkness. God desires that you walk in His light all your days so that darkness will not override your path. It is your covenant right to walk in the light of God. When you are confused and don't know or see clearly where you are going, it is time to declare your covenant right to divine illumination. Do not be afraid of darkness, but declare your right to the light of God, and you will see darkness flee before you. May the light of God always shine on your oath in all your days, in Jesus' name.

> PSALM 97:11 (KJV): *Light is sown for the righteous, and gladness for the upright in heart.*
>
> PROVERBS 4:18 (KJV): *But the path of the just is as the shining light, that shineth more and more unto the perfect day.*

The above Bible verses reveal that the Lord has planted His light in your life, so you should never walk in darkness. God has sown light in your life to keep darkness far away from your path. God desires that your path always shine brighter and brighter all your days. Therefore, it is your right to walk in the light of God.

Declare, as follows, your covenant right to divine illumination:

I am a child of God's covenant.

According to PSALM 97:11 and PROVERBS 4:18, it is my covenant right to walk in the light of God. Therefore, I claim my covenant right to divine illumination.

COVENANT RIGHT DECLARATION

I declare that in the light of God, I have light, in Jesus' name.

I declare that the lamp of God walks with me, and the candle of God dwells inside me, in Jesus' name.

I declare that I receive the light of God into my soul, body, and spirit, in Jesus' name.

I declare that I receive the light of God into my ways, in Jesus' name.

I declare that I receive the light of God to see all that God wants me to see, in Jesus' name.

I declare that I receive the light of God to see into the presence, future, every blind spot, and all that is hidden on my path, in Jesus' name.

I declare that I receive the light of God to detect and identify every opportunity the Lord sends my way, in Jesus' name.

I declare that I receive the light of God to detect and identify every secret plot of the wicked, including their hideouts, in my life, in Jesus' name.

I declare that I receive the light of God for clarification, interpretation, understanding, revelation, instruction, enlightenment, guidance, and counsel in all that concern me, in Jesus' name.

I declare that the light of God arises for me and enlightens my darkness, in Jesus' name.

I declare that the light of God shall bring me gladness, joy, and honour in all my days, in Jesus' name.

I declare that the light of God shall lead and bring me into the purpose of God always, in Jesus' name.

I declare that the light of God has made my path like a shining light that shines more and more unto the perfect day, in Jesus' name.

It is my covenant right to always walk in the light of God.

Therefore, I command the removal of any obstruction and veil hindering the light of God from reaching my life, in Jesus' name.

Any power sponsoring darkness in any area of my life, be broken in Jesus' name.

Whatever is in me that will not let the light of God shine in my life, die by fire, in Jesus' name.

Any area of my life where darkness is hanging, receive the light of God, in Jesus' name.

I decree that the light of God planted in my life will always shine, in Jesus' name.

It is my covenant right to experience divine illumination, and I shall always experience it in my life all my days, in Jesus' name.

Covenant-keeping God, I thank you because your covenant that gives me the right to enjoy your light has been established in my life and from today, I shall enjoy divine illumination in every area of life in all my days, in Jesus' name.

Additional Bible verses on divine illumination

JOB 22:28 (KJV): *Thou shalt also decree a thing, and it shall be established unto thee: and the light shall shine upon thy ways.*

PROVERBS 4:18 (KJV): *But the path of the just is as the shining light, that shineth more and more unto the perfect day.*

ISAIAH 60:1 (KJV): *Arise, shine; for thy light is come, and the glory of the LORD is risen upon thee.*

PROVERBS 13:9 (KJV): *The light of the righteous rejoiceth: but the lamp of the wicked shall be put out.*

PSALM 18:28 (KJV): *For thou wilt light my candle: the LORD my God will enlighten my darkness.*

CHAPTER TWENTY-SEVEN

COVENANT RIGHT DECLARATION
To Divine Restoration

God hates wastage and desires that whatever enemy has wasted in your life shall be restored to you. God wants to restore all that the enemy has stolen or destroyed in your life. Irrespective of how long the loss has taken place, God can restore to you all that you had lost to the enemy. It is your covenant right to enjoy the divine restoration of all your losses. When the enemy succeeds in stealing the blessings God has given you, then arise and declare your covenant right to divine restoration. Do not fold your hands and let the enemy go away with your blessings. Restoration of losses is your right, as it is detailed in the covenant word of God. May all your lost blessings be restored to you in many folds, in Jesus' name.

> Joel 2:25 (KJV): *And I will restore to you the years that the locust hath eaten, the cankerworm, and the caterpiller, and the palmerworm, my great army which I sent among you.*
>
> Jeremiah 30:17 (KJV): *For I will restore health unto thee, and I will heal thee of thy wounds, saith the LORD; because they called thee an Outcast, saying, This is Zion, whom no man seeketh after.*

In the above Bible verses, God promised to restore all we have lost to the enemy. The Lord will return all that the enemy has stolen from our lives. The Lord will not let our stolen blessings remain in the custody of the enemy forever. There shall be restoration.

If God has promised you restoration, it means you have been given the right to enjoy the restoration.

Therefore, it is your right to experience the restoration of your losses.

Whatever you might have lost to the enemy, either before or after you became born again, you have the right to claim it back from the enemy.

Declare, as follows, your covenant right to divine restoration:

I am a child of God's covenant.

According to JOEL 2:25 and JEREMIAH 30:17, it is my covenant right to enjoy the restoration of all my lost blessings.

Therefore, I claim my covenant right to divine restoration.

I declare that the Lord Jesus has made me righteous, justified me, and set me free from every condemnation.

I declare that the grace of God is upon me to claim back all my lost blessings in the custody of the enemy.

I declare that today, I claim back from the custody of the enemy all my lost and stolen blessings, in Jesus' name.

I declare that I repossess all the blessings the enemy has dispossessed me of, in Jesus' name.

I declare that I receive reinstatement into the position of honour I have lost, in Jesus' name.

I declare that I receive restitution and compensation for all my losses, in Jesus' name.

I declare that all my lost blessings in the custody of the enemy are hereby returned and reinstated to me, in Jesus' name.

I declare that every ruined and damaged area of my destiny is today rebuilt and repaired, in Jesus' name.

I claim into every area of my life the anointing for renewal, revival, rebuilding, refurbishment, recovery, and reformation, in Jesus' name.

I declare that I receive restoration of my lost vision, dream, hope, confidence, health, destiny, joy, peace, glory, power, productivity, fortune, position, honour, opportunities, and all the wasted years of my life, in Jesus' name.

I declare that my restoration is immediate, quick, timely, hastily, rapid, total, effective, without delay, and multifold, in Jesus' name.

The Lord has given me the right to restore all my wastes and losses, and I shall enjoy this restoration in all my days, in Jesus' name.

Therefore, any strongman that wants to stand in my way of restoration be destroyed now, in Jesus' name.

I command the angels of the Lord to clear the way for divine restoration in my life.

The Lord has given me the right to enjoy divine restoration, and I shall enjoy divine restoration in all the days of my life, in Jesus' name.

Covenant-keeping God, I thank you because your covenant that gives me the right to enjoy divine restoration has been established in my life. From today, I shall enjoy divine restoration in every area of life in all my days, in Jesus' name.

Additional Bible verses on divine restoration

ISAIAH 61:7 (KJV): *For your shame ye shall have double; and for confusion they shall rejoice in their portion: therefore in their land they shall possess the double: everlasting joy shall be unto them.*

PSALM 126:1 (KJV): *When the LORD turned again the captivity of Zion, we were like them that dream.*

JOB 42:10 (KJV): *And the LORD turned the captivity of Job, when he prayed for his friends: also the LORD gave Job twice as much as he had before.*

PROVERBS 6:30-31 (KJV): *Men do not despise a thief, if he steal to satisfy his soul when he is hungry; But if he be found, he shall restore sevenfold; he shall give all the substance of his house.*

ZECHARIAH 10:6 (KJV): *And I will strengthen the house of Judah, and I will save the house of Joseph, and I will bring them again to place them; for I have mercy upon them: and they shall be as though I had not cast them off: for I am the LORD their God, and will hear them.*

CHAPTER TWENTY-EIGHT

COVENANT RIGHT DECLARATION
To Live Above Condemnation

The Lord has justified and set you free from every condemnation and accusation. Your salvation gives you the right to live above every manner of condemnation. When the enemy attacks your mind with guilt and self-condemnation, it is time for you to start declaring your covenant right to live above condemnation. When you feel condemned by what you have done, remind yourself that it can't be God condemning you but the devil. Silent every voice of condemnation speaking to your mind by declaring your covenant right to live above condemnation. God has justified you, and no power or personality can condemn you. I pray for you that every voice that wants to accuse you will be permanently silenced, in Jesus' name.

> **ROMANS 8:1 (KJV):** *There is therefore now no condemnation to them which are in Christ Jesus, who walk not after the flesh, but after the Spirit.*
>
> **ROMANS 3:24 (KJV):** *Being justified freely by his grace through the redemption that is in Christ Jesus*

The above Bible verses clearly declare that you have been set free from any form of condemnation because you are in Christ Jesus.

Therefore, it is your covenant right to live above any form of condemnation and accusation. The Lord Jesus has justified you.

This implies that whoever is accusing or condemning you is violating the written word of God, and therefore, they are under God's wrath.

Declare, as follows, your covenant right to live above every condemnation:

I am a child of God's covenant.

According to ROMANS 8:1 and ROMANS 3:24, it is my covenant right to live above every condemnation.

Therefore, I claim my covenant right to live above every condemnation.

I declare that I am born of the Spirit of the Lord, and I dwell in Christ Jesus.

I declare that the grace of the Lord Jesus has set me free from the dominion of the law of sin and death, in Jesus' name.

I declare that the Lord Jesus has made me righteous and justified me in His name.

I declare that the Lord Jesus has sanctified me with His blood and word.

I declare that the gospel of the Lord Jesus has given me a new life and delivered me from every condemnation of the enemy.

I declare that I am an adopted child of God, a member of the heavenly family, in Jesus' name.

I declare that the Lord has pardoned me of every iniquity, both inherited and acquired, in Jesus' name.

I declare that the gospel of Jesus Christ has delivered me from every evil of this life and set me free from every accusation of the enemy.

I declare that I have been set free from every condemnation, accusation, judgement, disapproval, rejection, blame, reproach, sentence, sanction, curse, censure, damnation, charge, assault, criticism, fault-finding, conviction, objection, and all other consequences of iniquities, in Jesus' name.

I declare that I have been set free from every guilt, regret, and stain of sins, in Jesus' name.

There is no more condemnation for me because I am in Christ Jesus.

Therefore, I command to be cut off, any tongue and finger of accusation hired against me, in Jesus' name.

I command to shut down, any mouth of accusation opened against me in Jesus' name.

I command to go blind, any evil eye monitoring my life, in Jesus' name.

I command shame and reproach to all my accusers, in Jesus' name.

I command that all my faultfinders fall for my sake, in Jesus' name.

I command that every evil report of accusation written against me be consumed by fire, in Jesus' name.

I command any book of accusation that contains my name to catch fire in Jesus' name.

The Lord Jesus has set me free from every accusation and condemnation, and I shall live above every accusation and condemnation in all my days, in Jesus' name.

Covenant-keeping God, I thank you because your covenant that gives me the right to live above every condemnation has been established in my life. From today, I shall enjoy freedom from every form of condemnation in all my days in Jesus' name.

Additional Bible verses on living above condemnation

JOHN 5:24 (KJV): *Verily, verily, I say unto you, He that heareth my word, and believeth on him that sent me, hath everlasting life, and shall not come into condemnation; but is passed from death unto life.*

PHILIPPIANS 3:9 (KJV): *And be found in him, not having mine own righteousness, which is of the law, but that which is through the faith of Christ, the righteousness which is of God by faith:*

JOHN 3:18 (KJV): *He that believeth on him is not condemned: but he that believeth not is condemned already, because he hath not believed in the name of the only begotten Son of God.*

ROMANS 8:33-34 (KJV): *Who shall lay any thing to the charge of God's elect? It is God that justifieth. Who is he that condemneth? It is Christ that died, yea rather, that is risen again, who is even at the right hand of God, who also maketh intercession for us.*

PSALM 37:32-33 (KJV): *The wicked watcheth the righteous, and seeketh to slay him. The LORD will not leave him in his hand, nor condemn him when he is judged.*

CHAPTER TWENTY-NINE

COVENANT RIGHT DECLARATION
To Divine Satisfaction

God wants to satisfy you with every good thing. He wants you to live a life that is not limited by your needs. God wants to satisfy you with good health, favour, wisdom, direction, support, and every good thing you need for a glorious life. When it seems that good things are not enough in your life, it is time for you to start declaring your covenant right to divine satisfaction. Do not pass through life struggling to earn a decent living. Remember that for every good thing you need, the Lord has them in abundance. Therefore, don't let poverty or lack limit you. May you be satisfied with every good thing for a glorious life, in Jesus' name.

> **PSALM 65:4** (KJV): *Blessed is the man whom thou choosest, and causest to approach unto thee, that he may dwell in thy courts: we shall be satisfied with the goodness of thy house, even of thy holy temple.*
>
> **PSALM 36:8** (KJV): *They shall be abundantly satisfied with the fatness of thy house; and thou shalt make them drink of the river of thy pleasures.*

The above Bible verses assure us that as we come before God, we shall be satisfied with the goodness of God. We shall not lack or be in want of the good things of the Lord.

This assurance from the Lord guarantees you a life of satisfaction because of the goodness of God. This gives you the covenant right to enjoy the satisfaction of the good things of God.

Declare, as follows, your covenant right to divine satisfaction:

I am a child of God's covenant.

According to Psalm 65:4 and Psalm 36:8, my covenant right is to enjoy divine satisfaction.

Therefore, I claim my covenant right to divine satisfaction.

I declare I have a divine election, for the Lord has chosen me to be His child.

I declare that the Lord Jesus has justified me to approach the throne of God for His grace and mercy.

I declare I dwell in God and feed on His goodness, in Jesus' name.

I declare that all my needs are met in Christ Jesus.

I declare that I have abundant provisions from the Lord for all my spiritual needs, material needs, physical needs, psychological needs, emotional needs, financial needs, ministerial needs, social needs, mental needs, matrimonial needs, and all that my life requires for a glorious living, in Jesus' name.

I declare that in the Lord, my physiological needs are satisfied. I have abundant provision for food, shelter, clothing, sleep, and all other essential things I need for a decent living, in Jesus' name.

I declare that in the Lord, my safety needs are satisfied. I have abundant provision for my security needs for today and the future, in Jesus' name.

I declare that in the Lord, my social needs are satisfied. I have abundant provision for my need for love, affection, friendship, acceptance, and meaningful relationship, in Jesus' name.

I declare that in the Lord, my esteem needs are satisfied. I have abundant provision for my needs for self-respect, self-confidence, status, recognition, approval, and appreciation, in Jesus' name.

I declare that in the Lord, my self-actualisation needs are satisfied. I have abundant provision for my needs for self-development, self-awareness, self-discovery, and self-advancement, in Jesus' name.

I declare that in the Lord, all the needs I require to become the person God created me to be are satisfied, in Jesus' name.

I declare that in the Lord, I receive abundant provisions for my needs for grace, favour, power, wisdom, inspiration, understanding, knowledge, direction, fresh anointing, and every spiritual gift my destiny requires to flourish, in Jesus' name.

I declare that in the Lord, I receive abundant provision for all my seasonal needs, regular needs and occasional needs in Jesus' name.

I declare that in the Lord, all my needs are supplied timely, regularly, hastily and without delay, in Jesus' name.

It is my covenant right to enjoy divine satisfaction, and I shall enjoy it in all my days, in Jesus' name.

Covenant-keeping God, I thank you because your covenant that gives me the right to enjoy divine satisfaction has been established in my life. From today, I shall enjoy divine satisfaction in all my days, in Jesus' name.

Additional Bible verses on divine satisfaction

EXODUS 33:19 (KJV): *And he said, I will make all my goodness pass before thee, and I will proclaim the name of the LORD before thee; and will be gracious to whom I will be gracious, and will shew mercy on whom I will shew mercy.*

PSALM 63:5 (KJV): *My soul shall be satisfied as with marrow and fatness; and my mouth shall praise thee with joyful lips.*

JEREMIAH 31:12 (KJV): *Therefore they shall come and sing in the height of Zion, and shall flow together to the goodness of the LORD, for wheat, and for wine, and for oil, and for the young of the flock and of the herd: and their soul shall be as a watered garden; and they shall not sorrow any more at all.*

PSALM 17:15 (KJV): *As for me, I will behold thy face in righteousness: I shall be satisfied, when I awake, with thy likeness.*

NEHEMIAH 9:25 (KJV): *And they took strong cities, and a fat land, and possessed houses full of all goods, wells digged, vineyards, and oliveyards, and fruit trees in abundance: so they did eat, and were filled, and became fat, and delighted themselves in thy great goodness.*

CHAPTER THIRTY

COVENANT RIGHT DECLARATION
To Divine Wisdom

God is wiser than the wisest. It is in the plan of God to make you wiser than your enemies, so He has planted in you the spirit of wisdom. God has incorporated sound wisdom in His covenant, which the enemy can't overthrow. When it seems you lack idea and wise judgement about your life's situation, it is time for you to start declaring your covenant right to divine wisdom. When you do this, divine wisdom will suddenly rise within you as fresh ideas come to you from heaven. Do not let the ignorant take hold of you, but arise and declare your covenant right to the wisdom of God over the situation. May you be wiser than all your enemies in all your day, in Jesus' name.

> PROVERBS 2:7 (KJV): *He layeth up sound wisdom for the righteous: he is a buckler to them that walk uprightly.*
>
> COLOSSIANS 2:3 (KJV): *In whom are hid all the treasures of wisdom and knowledge.*

The above Bible verses say that the Lord has laid up sound wisdom for you to enjoy. He has given you the treasures of His wisdom.

It means that it is your covenant right to walk in the wisdom of God in all your ways.

Declare, as follows, your covenant right to divine wisdom:

I am a child of God's covenant.

According to PROVERB 2:7 and COLOSSIANS 2:3, it is my covenant right to enjoy sound wisdom from the Lord.

Therefore, I claim my covenant right to divine wisdom.

I declare that I am wise-hearted, and the wisdom of God dwells with me, in Jesus' name.

I declare that I have the wisdom of God to walk in discernment, good judgment, caution, intuition, enlightenment, foresight, understanding, and knowledge, in Jesus' name.

I declare that I have the wisdom of God to walk in the knowledge and fear of God, in Jesus' name.

I declare that I have the wisdom of God to walk uprightly and be blameless, in Jesus' name.

I declare that I have the wisdom of God to understand the mind of God in all that concerns me, in Jesus' name.

I declare that I have the wisdom of God to make profits and never make losses, in Jesus' name.

I declare that I have the wisdom of God to live a long life with good health, in Jesus' name.

I declare that I have the wisdom of God to live in protection and safety, in Jesus' name.

I declare that I have the wisdom of God to be strong and stay strong, in Jesus' name.

I declare that I have the wisdom of God to operate with the spirit of excellence and to do all things well in all my days, in Jesus' name.

I declare that I have the wisdom of God to differentiate between good and evil, fake and original, in Jesus' name.

I declare that I have the wisdom of God for godly vision and dream, in Jesus' name.

I declare that I have the wisdom of God to be rich and make others rich in Jesus' name.

I declare that I have the wisdom of God to earn favour from both men and God, in Jesus' name.

I declare that I have the wisdom of God to operate in dominion and to be established in destiny, in Jesus' name.

I declare that I have the wisdom of God for joyful and peaceful living, in Jesus' name.

I declare that I have the wisdom of God to walk in faith and confidence in the Lord, in Jesus' name.

I declare that I have the wisdom of God to live a glorious and honourable life, in Jesus' name.

I declare that I have the wisdom of God to be a voice for good and to shine in life, in Jesus' name.

I declare that I have the wisdom of God to build my house and establish my home, in Jesus' name.

I declare that I have the wisdom of God to fulfil the destiny and purpose of God for my life, in Jesus' name.

I declare that I have the wisdom of God to understand the mind of God in all that concerns me, in Jesus' name.

I declare that I have the wisdom of God to walk in victory and win all my battles, in Jesus' name.

I declare that I have the wisdom of God to live above every reproach and shame, in Jesus' name.

I declare that I have the wisdom of God to never fall into the trap of the wicked, in Jesus' name.

I declare that I have the wisdom of God to know and detect every hidden thing on my way, in Jesus' name.

I declare that I have the wisdom of God to access the secret of the Lord, in Jesus' name.

I declare that I have the wisdom of God to correctly judge every situation that comes my way, in Jesus' name.

I declare that I have the wisdom of God to detect and provoke my destiny helpers to help, in Jesus' name.

I declare that I have the wisdom of God to claim all that belongs to me from the custody of the enemy, in Jesus' name.

I declare that the wisdom of the Lord dwells with me, and I shall never fall into error or any traps of the wicked, in Jesus' name.

Therefore, I command every seed of foolish behaviour in me to die by fire in Jesus' name.

Covenant-keeping God, I thank you because your covenant that gives me the right to enjoy divine wisdom has been established in my life, and from today, I shall enjoy divine wisdom in all my days, in Jesus' name.

Additional Bible verses on divine wisdom

1 Corinthians 2:6 (KJV): *Howbeit we speak wisdom among them that are perfect: yet not the wisdom of this world, nor of the princes of this world, that come to nought.*

Proverbs 8:14 (KJV): *Counsel is mine, and sound wisdom: I am understanding; I have strength.*

Exodus 31:6 (KJV): *And I, behold, I have given with him Aholiab, the son of Ahisamach, of the tribe of Dan: and in the hearts of all that are wise hearted I have put wisdom, that they may make all that I have commanded thee.*

Ecclesiastes 7:12 (KJV): *For wisdom is a defence, and money is a defence: but the excellency of knowledge is, that wisdom giveth life to them that have it.*

Daniel 1:17 (KJV): *As for these four children, God gave them knowledge and skill in all learning and wisdom: and Daniel had understanding in all visions and dreams.*

BOOKS FROM THE SAME AUTHOR

Journey to the Next Level

The New Creature

Building a Glorious Home:
A Pathway to a Successful Marriage

Enemy of Marriage

Words That Heal

The Winning Formula

Faith that Always wins

Common Mistakes Parents make about their Children

Recovery is Possible
When you are desperate for a miracle

Decision
Path way to a wise decision making

Stop your fear before it stops you

The Visionary

This book, and all these other books from the same author, are available at Christian bookstores and distributors worldwide.

They can also be obtained through online retail partners such as Amazon or by contacting the author at the address below:

Address: 21-23 Stokes Croft, Bristol BS1 3PY United Kingdom

Email: kkasali@yahoo.com

Telephone: +44 (0) 7727 159 581

Milton Keynes UK
Ingram Content Group UK Ltd.
UKHW052233140224
437754UK00006BA/141